AQA
AS AND A LEVEL MUSIC

Listening Tests

PLAYBACK+
Speed • Pitch • Balance • Loop

To acces audio visit:
www.halleonardmgb.com/mylibrary

5449-4088-3329-6169

First published 2017 in Great Britain by
Rhinegold Education
14-15 Berners Street
London W1T 3LJ, UK
www.rhinegoldeducation.co.uk

© 2017 Rhinegold Education
a division of Wise Music Group

All rights reserved. No part of this publication may be reproduced, stored in a retrieval system, or transmitted in any form or by any means, electronic, mechanical, photocopying, recording or otherwise, without the prior permission of Rhinegold Education.

Rhinegold Education has used its best efforts in preparing this guide. It does not assume, and hereby disclaims, any liability to any party for loss or damage caused by errors or omissions in the guide whether such errors or omissions result from negligence, accident or other cause.

> You should always check the current requirements of your examination, since these may change.

Editor: Lucy Metzger and Katharine Allenby
Cover and book design: Fresh Lemon Australia

AQA AS and A LEVEL Music Listening Tests
Order no. RHG141
ISBN 978-1-78558-156-4

Exclusive Distributors:
Hal Leonard Europe Limited
Newmarket Road
Bury St Edmunds IP33 3YB

Printed in the EU

Available from Rhinegold Education for your course:
- **AQA AS and A Level Music Study Guide**
- **AQA AS Level Music Revision Guide**
- **AQA A Level Music Revision Guide**

You may find the following books useful too:
- **AS Music Harmony Workbook**
- **A2 Music Harmony Workbook**
- **AS Music Composition Workbook**
- **AS Music Literacy Workbook**
- **Writing About Music Workbook**
- **Understanding Popular Music**
- **Careers in Music**
- **Music Technology from Scratch**
- **Dictionary of Music in Sound**

AQA
AS AND A LEVEL MUSIC

Listening Tests

**CHRIS FISH &
MARK WILDERSPIN**

The authors

Chris Fish
read music at Magdalene College, Cambridge. He currently teaches at Alleyn's School in Dulwich and was previously Head of Music at The American School in Switzerland. He is a senior examiner and A Level advisor. His compositions and arrangements (often for his barbershop quartet, Barbershop-o-gram) have been performed on national television and radio. He lives in south-west London with his partner and two young daughters.

Mark Wilderspin
read music at The Queen's College, Oxford, and was a postgraduate scholar at the Royal College of Music, where he studied composition for screen. Since then he has dovetailed teaching with a freelance career that has seen him working on Hollywood feature films and scoring for clients such as Historic Royal Palaces and the BBC. For Rhinegold Publishing he was a co-author of the *Elements* series of books, and author of *Danny Elfman's Batman in Focus.* He is currently Director of Music at St Paul's School, London, and an A Level examiner.

Contents

Introduction 6

AS Level tests 15

Full paper 15
Additional dictation questions 43
Additional Section B questions 45

A Level tests 54

Full paper 54
Additional dictation questions 91
Additional Section B questions 93

Optional Areas of Study (AoS): additional questions 112

Area of Study 2:
Pop music 112

Area of Study 3:
Music for media 115

Area of Study 4:
Music for theatre 118

Area of Study 5:
Jazz 121

Area of Study 6:
Contemporary traditional music 124

Area of Study 7:
Art music since 1910 127

Answers 130

Track listings and copyrights 143

Introduction to the AQA AS and A Level Listening Paper

If you are reading this introduction you are probably either studying or teaching AS or A Level music. Whichever category you fall into, you will almost certainly favour certain genres of music over others. This new specification is designed to recognise and celebrate these preferences and whereas in the previous AQA Specification you could follow your own pathway only in performing and composition, now you can also do so in Component 1: Appraising music.

Your choice lies in the optional Areas of Study, which are laid out in the table opposite. At AS Level you choose one Area of Study and at A Level you choose two. These are examined in Sections A and C of the Unit 1 examination.

Section B of the examination tests your knowledge of the **compulsory** Area of Study, Western Classical tradition 1650–1910. This Area of Study also appears in Section A of the examination.

What is in the examination paper?

The examination will include unfamiliar music (Section A), set works (Section B) and essay questions (Section C – not included in this book of listening tests).

The unfamiliar music will always be from the named genres (Area of Study 1) and named artists/composers (Areas of Study 2 to 7). All of these genres and artists/composers are named in Table 1. (AQA have published a list of suggested listening for Areas of Study 2 to 7. These are listed in the Study Guide published by Rhinegold Education and on the AQA website. NOTE: these pieces of suggested listening WILL NOT feature in Section A of the examination.)

> For detail about the representative repertoire suggested by AQA for each AoS, see the Study Guide published by Rhinegold Education.

Table 1 Areas of Study (AoS) for AS and A Level Music

Compulsory Area of Study

Area of Study	AS Level	A Level
AoS 1: Western Classical tradition 1650–1910	Two strands: - Baroque solo concerto - The operas of Mozart	Three strands: - Baroque solo concerto - The operas of Mozart - The piano music of Chopin, Brahms and Grieg

Optional Areas of Study

AS Level Music: choose **ONE** area from AoS 2 to 6.
A Level Music: choose **TWO** areas from AoS 2 to 7.

AoS 2: Pop music	- Stevie Wonder - Joni Mitchell - Muse	- Beyoncé - Daft Punk - Labrinth
AoS 3: Music for media	- Bernard Herrmann - Hans Zimmer - Michael Giacchino	- Thomas Newman - Nobuo Uematsu
AoS 4: Music for theatre	- Kurt Weill - Richard Rodgers - Stephen Sondheim	- Claude-Michel Schönberg - Jason Robert Brown
AoS 5: Jazz	- Louis Armstrong - Duke Ellington - Charlie Parker	- Miles Davis - Pat Metheny - Gwilym Simcock
AoS 6: Contemporary traditional music	- Astor Piazzolla - Toumani Diabaté - Anoushka Shankar	- Mariza - Bellowhead

A Level only

AoS 7: Art music since 1910	- Dmitri Shostakovich - Olivier Messiaen	- Steve Reich - James MacMillan

AS/A LEVEL MUSIC LISTENING TESTS

The structure of the AQA question papers

By offering so many different Areas of Study, AQA has made sure that there is 'something for everyone'. However, there will be a large number of questions on the examination paper, and you will be answering only some of these. Navigating the paper will be an important element of exam technique and may prove a challenge in itself!

The structure of the AS Level paper is shown in Table 2, and the structure of the A Level paper is shown in Table 3. Familiarise yourself with this scheme – it will help you feel settled in the examination.

N.B. The question numbers will be the same EVERY YEAR so you can learn which ones you will answer, and which ones you will leave out (this, of course, will be the majority!).

You will control your own audio in the exam and decide how many times to listen to each excerpt of music. The examination paper will give *suggested* timings for how long you may wish to spend on each section of the exam.

Table 2 Structure of AS Level Music examination paper, Component 1: Appraising music

SECTION A Listening

Suggested time: 50 minutes

AoS 1 is compulsory, and you will be asked to answer **four questions** on it. You will also be asked to choose **ONE** further AoS and answer **four questions** on that, so for Section A you will answer **eight questions** in all.

Area of Study	Question no.	Type of question	Marks	Total marks

AoS 1 – Compulsory: answer **ALL FOUR** questions.

Area of Study	Question no.	Type of question	Marks	Total marks
AoS 1: Western Classical tradition 1650–1910	1	Excerpt of Baroque music, short answer questions	4	Total marks for AoS 1: 24
	2	Excerpt of Classical music, short answer questions	4	
	3	Aural dictation question, Baroque or Classical music	6	
	4	Long answer, choosing excerpt from either question 1 or question 2 and commenting on Baroque or Classical features	10	

AoS 2 to 6 – In only **ONE** AoS (your chosen area), answer **ALL FOUR** questions.

Area of Study	Question no.	Type of question	Marks	Total marks
AoS 2: Pop music	5	Excerpt of representative repertoire, short answer questions	5	Total marks for AoS 2: 25
	6	Excerpt of representative repertoire, short answer questions	5	
	7	Excerpt of representative repertoire, short answer questions	5	
	8	Excerpt of representative repertoire, long answer question	10	

AoS 3: Music for media	9	Excerpt of representative repertoire, short answer questions	5	
	10	Excerpt of representative repertoire, short answer questions	5	
	11	Excerpt of representative repertoire, short answer questions	5	**Total marks for AoS 3: 25**
	12	Excerpt of representative repertoire, long answer question	10	
AoS 4: Music for theatre	13	Excerpt of representative repertoire, short answer questions	5	
	14	Excerpt of representative repertoire, short answer questions	5	
	15	Excerpt of representative repertoire, short answer questions	5	**Total marks for AoS 4: 25**
	16	Excerpt of representative repertoire, long answer question	10	
AoS 5: Jazz	17	Excerpt of representative repertoire, short answer questions	5	
	18	Excerpt of representative repertoire, short answer questions	5	
	19	Excerpt of representative repertoire, short answer questions	5	**Total marks for AoS 5: 25**
	20	Excerpt of representative repertoire, long answer question	10	
AoS 6: Contemporary traditional music	21	Excerpt of representative repertoire, short answer questions	5	
	22	Excerpt of representative repertoire, short answer questions	5	
	23	Excerpt of representative repertoire, short answer questions	5	**Total marks for AoS 6: 25**
	24	Excerpt of representative repertoire, long answer question	10	

Total marks for Section A: 49

SECTION B Analysis (of set works)

Suggested time: 25 minutes

Answer **EITHER** question 25 **OR** question 26.

Area of Study	Question no.	Type of question	Marks
AoS 1: Western Classical tradition 1650–1910	25	Excerpt from a Baroque solo concerto set work, short answer questions (totalling 7 marks) and one long answer question (10 marks)	17
	26	Excerpt from a Mozart opera set work, short answer questions (totalling 7 marks) and one long answer question (10 marks)	17
			Total marks for Section B: 17

SECTION C Essay

Suggested time: 45 minutes

Answer **ONE** essay question in your chosen Area of Study.

Area of Study	Question no.	Type of question	Marks
AoS 2: Pop music	27	Essay question	30
AoS 3: Music for media	28	Essay question	30
AoS 4: Music for theatre	29	Essay question	30
AoS 5: Jazz	30	Essay question	30
AoS 6: Contemporary traditional music	31	Essay question	30
			Total marks for Section C: 30

Total time for AS paper: 2 hours **Total marks for AS paper: 96**

INTRODUCTION

Table 3 Structure of A Level Music examination paper, Component 1: Appraising music

SECTION A Listening

Suggested time: 65 minutes

AoS 1 is compulsory, and you will be asked to answer **three questions** on it. You will also be asked to choose **TWO** further AoS and answer **three questions on each**, so for Section A you will answer **nine questions** in all.

Area of Study	Question no.	Type of question	Marks	Total marks
AoS 1 – Compulsory: answer **ALL THREE** questions.				
AoS 1: Western Classical tradition 1650–1910	1	Excerpt from one of the three strands, short answer questions	4	Total marks for AoS 1: 20
	2	Aural dictation question based on another of the three strands	6	
	3	Excerpt from the remaining strand, long answer question	10	
AoS 2 to 6 – In **TWO** AoS (your chosen areas), answer **ALL FOUR** questions.				
AoS 2: Pop music	4	Excerpt of representative repertoire, short answer questions	4	Total marks for AoS 2: 18
	5	Excerpt of representative repertoire, short answer questions	4	
	6	Excerpt of representative repertoire, long answer question	10	
AoS 3: Music for media	7	Excerpt of representative repertoire, short answer questions	4	Total marks for AoS 3: 18
	8	Excerpt of representative repertoire, short answer questions	4	
	9	Excerpt of representative repertoire, long answer question	10	
AoS 4: Music for theatre	10	Excerpt of representative repertoire, short answer questions	4	Total marks for AoS 4: 18
	11	Excerpt of representative repertoire, short answer questions	4	
	12	Excerpt of representative repertoire, long answer question	10	

AS/A LEVEL MUSIC LISTENING TESTS

Area of Study	Question no.	Type of question	Marks	
AoS 5: Jazz	13	Excerpt of representative repertoire, short answer questions	4	
	14	Excerpt of representative repertoire, short answer questions	4	**Total marks for AoS 5: 18**
	15	Excerpt of representative repertoire, long answer question	10	
AoS 6: Contemporary traditional music	16	Excerpt of representative repertoire, short answer questions	4	
	17	Excerpt of representative repertoire, short answer questions	4	**Total marks for AoS 6: 18**
	18	Excerpt of representative repertoire, long answer question	10	
AoS 7: Art music since 1910	19	Excerpt of representative repertoire, short answer questions	4	
	20	Excerpt of representative repertoire, short answer questions	4	**Total marks for AoS 7: 18**
	21	Excerpt of representative repertoire, long answer question	10	

Total marks for Section A: 36

SECTION B Analysis and context (of set works)

Suggested time: 40 minutes

Answer **TWO** of the three questions given.

Area of Study	Question no.	Type of question	Marks
AoS 1: Western Classical tradition 1650–1910	22	Excerpt from a Baroque solo concerto set work, short answer questions (totalling 2 marks), medium length questions (totalling 5 marks) and one long answer question (10 marks)	17
	23	Excerpt from a Mozart opera set work, short answer questions (totalling 2 marks), medium length questions (totalling 5 marks) and one long answer question (10 marks)	17
	24	Excerpt from a piece of 19th-century piano music set work, short answer questions (totalling 2 marks), medium length questions (totalling 5 marks) and one long answer question (10 marks)	17

Total marks for Section B: 34

SECTION C Essay
Suggested time: 45 minutes

Answer **ONE** essay question in **ONE** of your two chosen Areas of Study.

Area of Study	Question no.	Type of question	Marks
AoS 2: Pop music	25	Essay question	30
AoS 3: Music for media	26	Essay question	30
AoS 4: Music for theatre	27	Essay question	30
AoS 5: Jazz	28	Essay question	30
AoS 6: Contemporary traditional music	29	Essay question	30
AoS 7: Art music since 1910	30	Essay question	30

Total marks for Section C: 30

Total time for A Level paper: 2½ hours   **Total marks for A Level paper: 120**

What to expect in AS and A Level questions

Section A

As mentioned above, Section A will contain excerpts of music which are unfamiliar. As shown in Tables 2 and 3, there will be short answers, aural dictation and longer answers.

The short answer questions will focus on a variety of features that may be heard in the excerpt (e.g. harmonic or melodic intervals, cadences, tonality, rhythm etc.). In the optional Areas of Study, each set of questions will contain a question that uses notation in some form.

The dictation questions (which will always be question 3 in the AS exam and question 2 in the A Level exam) will require **six** notes to be added. These are unlikely to be in a single block of six notes. At AS, only the treble clef will be used. At A Level there will be a mixture of treble and bass clef gaps to be filled.

Long answer questions will require contextual knowledge to be incorporated into the answer.

Section B

Section B is based entirely on the set works from Area of Study 1 (for exact details see both the Rhinegold Education Study Guide and the AQA website). You will be given both sheet music and recordings for the excerpts. You will be able to refer to both in order to answer the questions.

The short answer questions will be similar in nature to those in Section A.

AS/A LEVEL MUSIC LISTENING TESTS

The long answer questions will once again require contextual knowledge to be displayed in order to gain top marks.

Section C
Don't forget that in this section you will have to write an essay on one of your optional Areas of Study. There are no examples of essays in this book. By listening to pieces and practising the skills needed to answer the essay questions in Section C you will also be reinforcing the aural skills needed to do well in Sections A and B.

How to use this book

Because of the complicated structure of the exam, we have included a 'sample' paper for both AS and A Level. The question numbers, types of questions and choices of excerpts are our best effort to recreate what you might expect in the final examination.

We have also included further questions on each of the Areas of Study. These all represent the same number of marks, which will help you to compare how you are faring in each different Area of Study.

It is tempting to think that only a small section of the questions contained in this book are applicable to you – you have chosen one or two optional Areas of Study, so you don't need to bother with the other four or five.

We would recommend, however, that you make use of those questions as well; though the artists or composers and genres will not be ones you are totally familiar with, the listening skills covered are fundamentally the same in each Area of Study. (The exception will be where the question deals with specific features of a genre; to enable the book to be flexible, we have kept these types of question to relatively few.)

Top tips to maximise marks

Be clear
Good spelling and grammar are important. Why? Put simply, spelling and grammar are ways in which we standardise the written word: with good grammar and spelling, meaning is clear and unambiguous. This is clearly an advantage – you do not want an examiner desperately trying to decipher what you mean.

Be concise
Correct and appropriate use of musical terms is also vital to being clear and concise.
Take the following example:

'The melody starts on one note and then moves by step up one note then returns to the original note.'

OR

'The melody uses an upper auxiliary note.'

Clearly, the second is preferable in a pressured, timed examination!

Be neat
When writing musical notes in the dictation questions, use a pencil, or better still write in rough first. Be precise when drawing notes – do not, for example, go onto a line if you are trying to write in a space.

If you need to cross out an answer, do so in as unobtrusive a manner as you can.

In short – help the examiner to glean the information you are trying to convey. That way you will be sure of gaining the marks you have worked so hard to achieve!

AS Level tests

AS Level full paper

Section A: Listening

50 minutes – 49 marks

Answer **all four** questions in Area of Study 1 and **all four** questions in **one** other Area of Study 2 to 6.

Area of Study 1: Western Classical tradition 1650–1910

Spend 25 minutes on this section.

Question 1 is on the excerpt of music on track 1
Question 2 is on the excerpt of music on track 2
Question 3 is on the excerpt of music on track 3
Question 4 is a choice of music on track 4a or track 4b – Baroque characteristics or Classical characteristics

Question 1

Track 1 (Baroque)

1.1 What is the tonality of the excerpt?

[1 mark]

1.2 The opening motif is repeated at 0:08. How much higher is the pitch?

[1 mark]

1.3 Name the ornament played by the solo instrument when it is heard alone for the second time.

[1 mark]

1.4 Describe how the rhythm of the solo line changes leading up to the cadence at the end of the excerpt.

[1 mark]

Total: 4 marks

Question 2

Track 2 (Classical)

2.1 Which of the following best describes the chord at the opening of the excerpt? Underline your answer.

major   **minor**   **augmented**   **diminished** [1 mark]

2.2 Which voice type is the singer?

_____ [1 mark]

2.3 Write out the repeated rhythmic pattern heard in the accompaniment while the singer sings.

[2 marks]

Total: 4 marks

Question 3

Track 3

Complete the melody in the bracketed sections of this aria by Mozart.
The rhythm is given above the stave.

Total: 6 marks

Question 4

Track 4a (Baroque) or 4b (Classical)

Choose **one** of the excerpts heard in track 4a (Baroque) or track 4b (Classical).

Explain which features of the music help you to identify that it is from the Baroque or Classical period.

Total: 10 marks

AS/A LEVEL MUSIC LISTENING TESTS

Answer **all four** questions for **one** Area of Study 2 to 6.

Area of Study 2: Pop music

Spend 25 minutes on this section.

Question 5 is on the excerpt of music on track 5
Question 6 is on the excerpt of music on track 6
Question 7 is on the excerpt of music on track 7
Question 8 is on the excerpt of music on track 8

Question 5

Track 5

The excerpt is from Stevie Wonder's 'My cherie amour'. The lyrics for the excerpt are below.

INTRO
1   La la la la la la, La la la la la la

VERSE 1
2   My cherie amour, lovely as a summer day
3   My cherie amour, distant as the milky way
4   My cherie amour, pretty little one that I adore
5   You're the only girl my heart beats for
6   How I wish that you were mine

5.1 Which of the following melodic contours fits the first six notes of flute melody in the Intro? Tick your answer.

A

B

C

D

[1 mark]

5.2 What is the time signature of this excerpt?

[1 mark]

5.3 What is the compass of line 2 (the first line of the VERSE)?

[1 mark]

5.4 Line 4 has the same initial shape as line 2. How much higher does it start?

[1 mark]

5.5 What is the tonality of this excerpt?

[1 mark]

Total: 5 marks

Question 6

Track 6

The excerpt is from Muse's 'MK ultra'. The lyrics of the excerpt are below.

1 How much deception can you take?
2 How many lies will you create?
3 How much longer until you break?
4 Your mind's about to fall

5 And they're breaking through
6 They're breaking through
7 They're breaking through
8 We are losing control

6.1 What is the harmonic device heard in the middle of the texture in the first three lines?

[1 mark]

6.2 What is the interval between the two vocal lines on the word 'fall' (underlined)?

[1 mark]

6.3 Identify the rhythm of the bass riff from line 5 onwards by ticking the correct rhythm below.

A

B

C

D

[1 mark]

6.4 Name **TWO** instruments playing (apart from vocals and bass guitar).

[2 marks]

Total: 5 marks

Question 7

Track 7

You will hear the intro and first lyrics from 'Instant crush' by Daft Punk. The lyrics of the excerpt are below.

1 I didn't want to be the one to forget
2 I thought of everything I'd never regret
3 A little time with you is all that I get
4 That's all we need because it's all we can take

7.1 What type of cadence leads into the first vocal entry?

_____ [1 mark]

7.2 What type of chord is heard in the accompaniment to line 2?

_____ [1 mark]

7.3 What is the vocal compass of lines 1 and 2?

_____ [1 mark]

7.4 Identify **TWO** features of this excerpt. Underline your answers.

vocals fed into a vocoder   **sampled vocals**

repeated chord sequence   **shaker ostinato**   **inverted pedal**   [2 marks]

Total: 5 marks

Question 8

Track 8

The excerpt is from 'Halo' by Beyoncé. The lyrics of the excerpt are below.

1 It's like I've been awakened
2 Every rule I had you breaking
3 The risk that I'm taking
4 I'm never gonna shut you out

5 Everywhere I'm looking now
6 I'm surrounded by your embrace
7 Baby I can see your halo
8 You know you're my saving grace

9 You're everything I need and more
10 It's written all over your face
11 Baby I can feel your halo
12 Pray it won't fade away

13 I can feel your halo halo halo
14 I can see your halo halo halo
15 I can feel your halo halo halo
16 I can see your halo halo halo

As well as being a down-tempo R'n'B song, this song has gospel and soul influences. Explain how the musical elements exemplify aspects of these three different styles.

Total: 10 marks

Area of Study 3: Music for media

Spend 25 minutes on this section.

Question 9 is on the excerpt of music on track 9
Question 10 is on the excerpt of music on track 10
Question 11 is on the excerpt of music on track 11
Question 12 is on the excerpt of music on track 12

Question 9

Track 9

The excerpt is from Thomas Newman's score to *Erin Brockovich*. The cue is called 'Miss Wichita'.

9.1 What type of chord is heard just before the solo melody begins?

[1 mark]

9.2 Which of the following outlines represents the first six notes of the solo melody? Tick your answer.

[1 mark]

9.3 What string technique can be heard in this excerpt?

[1 mark]

9.4 What harmonic device is heard throughout this excerpt?

[1 mark]

9.5 What is the tonality of the excerpt?

[1 mark]

Total: 5 marks

AS LEVEL TESTS

Question 10

Track 10

The excerpt is from Bernard Herrmann's score to *The Snows of Kilimanjaro*.

10.1 The opening melody is shown here with two blank bars. Circle the **TWO BARS** that may be repeated to fill in the blank bars and complete the melody.

etc. [2 marks]

10.2 Name **ONE** instrument playing the melody.

[1 mark]

10.3 Name the instrument accompanying the melody.

[1 mark]

10.4 By which dance form is this music inspired? Underline your answer.

march   **minuet**   **gigue**   **waltz**   [1 mark]

Total: 5 marks

Question 11

Track 11

The excerpt is from Hans Zimmer's score to *True Romance*. The cue is called 'You're so cool'.

11.1 What is the interval between the two notes of the melody from 0:00–0:04?

[1 mark]

11.2 What is the tonality of this excerpt?

[1 mark]

11.3 Name the untuned percussion instrument being synthesised at 0:38 and heard continuously until the end of the extract.

[1 mark]

11.4 Which **TWO** of the following are features of this excerpt? Underline your answers.

pedal   **delay effect**   **cross rhythm**   **canon**   **trill**   [2 marks]

Total: 5 marks

Question 12

Track 12

The excerpt is from Michael Giacchino's score to the video game *The Lost World: Jurassic Park*. The cue is called 'Laboratory hunt'. In this level of the game, the player controls a carnivorous dinosaur that hunts down armed guards who are attempting to prevent its escape from a laboratory.

Explain how the use of musical elements in the excerpt creates a suitable atmosphere for this level of the game.

Total: 10 marks

Area of Study 4: Music for theatre

Spend 25 minutes on this section.

Question 13 is on the excerpt of music on track 13

Question 14 is on the excerpt of music on track 14

Question 15 is on the excerpt of music on track 15

Question 16 is on the excerpt of music on track 16

Question 13

Track 13

The excerpt is from Rodgers and Hammerstein's *Oklahoma!* The song is 'People will say we're in love' (beginning just before the first refrain). The lyrics for the excerpt are below.

1 Here is the gist, a practical list of *don'ts* for you

REFRAIN

2 Don't throw bouquets at me
3 Don't please my folks too much
4 Don't laugh at my jokes too much
5 People will say we're in love

13.1 Which of the following describes the harmony at the moment 'you' (underlined above) is heard? Underline your answer.

root position minor chord   **root position major chord**

first inversion major chord   **first inversion minor chord**   [1 mark]

13.2 Describe the melody played in a high register at the end of each phrase of the refrain.

_____ [1 mark]

13.3 What is the interval between the lyrics 'folks' and 'too' (underlined above)?

_____ [1 mark]

13.4 What is the main similarity between the first three phrases of the refrain?

_____ [1 mark]

13.5 What is the repeated interval in the final phrase of the excerpt?

_____ [1 mark]

Total: 5 marks

Question 14

Track 14

The excerpt is from Stephen Sondheim's *A Little Night Music*. The song is 'Send in the clowns'.

1 Isn't it rich?
2 Are we a pair?
3 Me here at last on the ground
4 You in midair
5 Send in the clowns

14.1 Other than the orchestral strings, name **TWO** instruments you can hear in the excerpt.

[2 marks]

14.2 On which word is the melody first doubled in the orchestra?

[1 mark]

14.3 Which of the following shapes represents the melody on the lyric 'you in midair'?
Tick your answer.

A

B

C

D

[1 mark]

14.4 On which lyric is the highest note of the melody sung?

[1 mark]

Total: 5 marks

Question 15

Track 15

The excerpt is from Kurt Weill's *Street Scene*. The song is 'Wrapped in a ribbon and tied in a bow'.

1 We sat in our snowy-white dresses
2 And then it was my turn to go
3 'Your diploma', they said, and I took it
4 Wrapped in a ribbon and tied in a bow
5 I felt like it must feel in heaven

15.1 What cadence is heard at the lyric 'tied in a bow'?

[1 mark]

15.2 Name the interval between the highest and lowest melodic notes.

[1 mark]

15.3 On the line below, write the one-bar repeated rhythm of the double bass in the excerpt.

‖ 4/4 _____ |

[2 marks]

15.4 Name the playing technique used by the double bass in the excerpt.

[1 mark]

Total: 5 marks

Question 16

Track 16

The excerpt is from Boublil and Schönberg's *Les Misérables*. The scene is called 'Confrontation'. Javert, a policeman, is attempting to take Valjean (who sings first), a convicted felon who has broken his parole terms, back into custody. Valjean, however, has vowed to another character that he will save her daughter and he wants to fulfil this promise before turning himself in.

Explain how the musical elements add a sense of drama to the scene.

Total: 10 marks

Area of Study 5: Jazz

Spend 25 minutes on this section.

Question 17 is on the excerpt of music on track 17
Question 18 is on the excerpt of music on track 18
Question 19 is on the excerpt of music on track 19
Question 20 is on the excerpt of music on track 20

Question 17

Track 17

The excerpt is from Duke Ellington's 'Take the A-Train'.

17.1 Which series of notes is played at the opening of the excerpt? Tick your answer.

A

B

C

D

[1 mark]

17.2 This series of notes is repeated. Give one difference between the first and second times it is heard.

_____ [1 mark]

17.3 When the main melody begins, how long is the first note?

_____ [1 mark]

17.4 Which chord can be heard at 0:30?

_____ [1 mark]

17.5 Which of the following best represents the structure of the excerpt? Underline your answer.

Intro 12-bar blues   **Intro ABAB**   **Intro AABA**   **Intro ABCA**   [1 mark]

Total: 5 marks

Question 18

Track 18

The excerpt is from Miles Davis's album *Birth of the Cool*. The track is called 'Move'.

18.1 What is the repeated melodic interval at 0:07?

[1 mark]

18.2 Which **TWO** instruments play this melody?

[2 marks]

18.3 How many beats are there before the main melody begins?

[1 mark]

18.4 Describe the dynamics of the chord just before the trumpet solo begins.

[1 mark]

Total: 5 marks

Question 19

Track 19

The excerpt is from Charlie Parker's track 'Ornithology' from the album of the same name.

19.1 Insert the **TWO** accidentals that have been omitted from the first bar of the melody.

[2 marks]

19.2 How many individual instruments can be heard in the excerpt?

[1 mark]

19.3 Give an appropriate metronome mark for the excerpt.

[1 mark]

19.4 Which of the following describes the first chord in the excerpt? Underline your answer.

    tritone substitution   major   augmented   half-diminished   [1 mark]

Total: 5 marks

Question 20

Track 20

The excerpt is from Pat Metheny's album *Letter from Home*. The track is called 'Spring ain't here'.

Explain how this track combines typical jazz features with elements from outside jazz.

Total: 10 marks

Area of Study 6: Contemporary traditional music

Spend 25 minutes on this section.

Question 21 is on the excerpt of music on track 21
Question 22 is on the excerpt of music on track 22
Question 23 is on the excerpt of music on track 23
Question 24 is on the excerpt of music on track 24

Question 21

Track 21

The excerpt is from the song 'Jordan' by Bellowhead. The lyrics of the excerpt are below.

1 Thunder in the clouds, lightning in the trees
2 What do you think that I told him?
3 It's goodbye, Sam, till the next kingdom come
4 And I'll meet you on the other side of Jordan

CHORUS

5 Pull off your old coat and roll up your sleeves
6 Jordan is a hard road to travel, I believe

21.1 On what degree of the scale does the vocal enter?

[1 mark]

21.2 What is the compass of the melody of lines 1 and 2?

[1 mark]

21.3 What vocal technique is heard in the underlined part of line 3?

[1 mark]

21.4 The chorus (line 5) begins on which chord? Underline your answer.

    dominant   **mediant**   **subdominant**   **submediant**   [1 mark]

21.5 What is the vocal texture of line 6 in the chorus?

[1 mark]

Total: 5 marks

AS LEVEL TESTS

Question 22

Track 22

The excerpt is from the song 'Rosa Branca' by Mariza

22.1 Apart from the tonic (G) on the downbeat, what are the other **TWO** notes of the riff heard several times at the start of the excerpt?

_____

_____ [2 marks]

22.2 Apart from chord I, what other chord is heard in the first four short vocal phrases?

_____ [1 mark]

22.3 The excerpt begins in G major. In what key does it end?

_____ [1 mark]

22.4 Which of the following is **NOT** a feature of this excerpt? Underline your answer.

    grace notes   **circle of 5ths**   **drone**   **dominant 9th**   [1 mark]

Total: 5 marks

Question 23

Track 23

The excerpt is from Anoushka Shankar's song 'Reunion' from the album *Land of Gold*.

23.1 Name the **TWO** Western instruments heard in this excerpt.

_____

_____ [2 marks]

23.2 Suggest a suitable tempo for the excerpt.

_____ [1 mark]

23.3 What is the range of the melody before the entry of the percussion instrument?

_____ [1 mark]

23.4 The excerpt is based on a repeated chord progression. How many chords does it contain? Underline your answer.

    six   **seven**   **eight**   **nine**   [1 mark]

Total: 5 marks

Question 24

Track 24

The excerpt is from the album *Boulevard de l'Independance* by Toumani Diabaté's Symmetric Orchestra. The track is called 'Ya fama'.

Explain how Toumani Diabaté and his fellow musicians blend traditional West African music with other styles in this excerpt.

Total: 10 marks

Section B: Analysis (set works)
25 minutes – 17 marks

Answer **ONE** question from questions 25-26.

The music for question 25 is on track 25

The music for question 26 is on track 26

Score excerpts are provided below.

Question 25

Track 25 Baroque solo concerto

This excerpt is from a Vivaldi solo concerto. Answer the following questions, which are based on the score excerpt printed below.

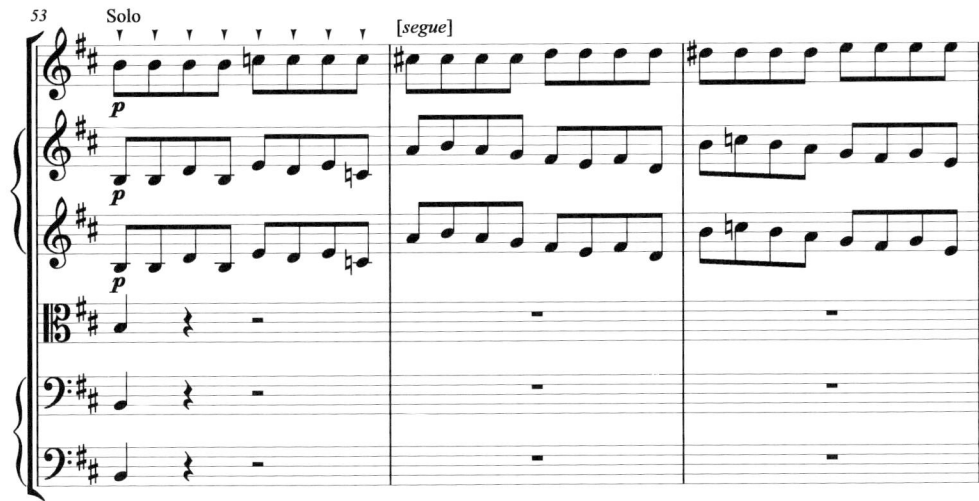

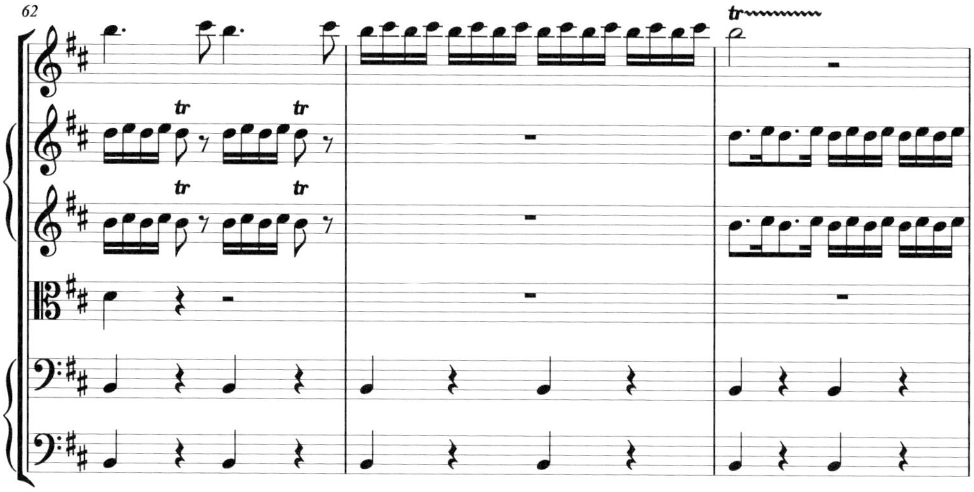
62
tr
tr
tr
tr
tr

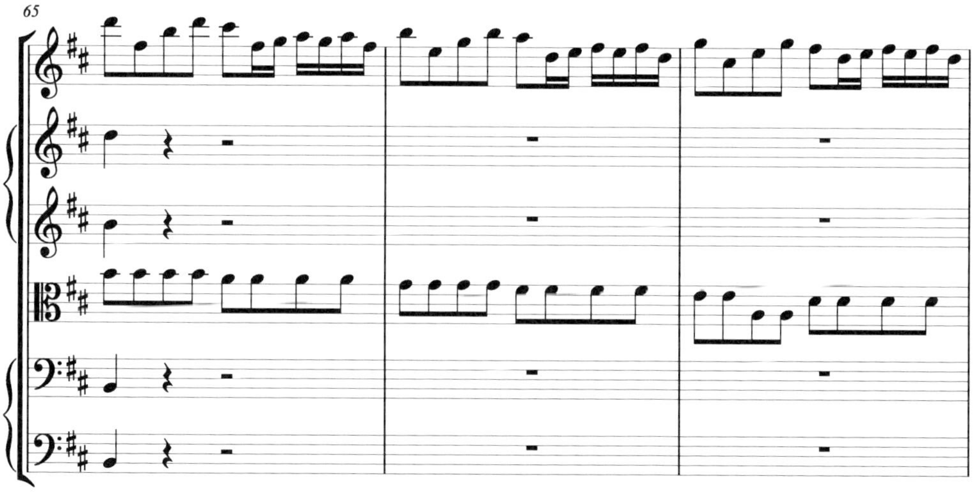
65

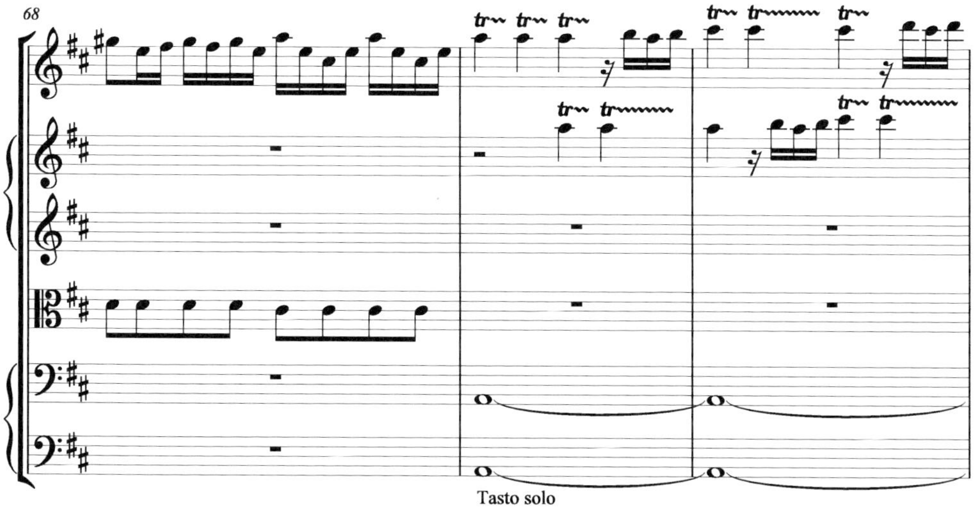
68
tr tr tr
tr tr tr
tr tr
tr tr
Tasto solo

AS/A LEVEL MUSIC LISTENING TESTS

25.1 What significance does the theme heard at the opening of the excerpt have in the context of this concerto movement?

[1 mark]

25.2 What is the key in bar 55?

[1 mark]

25.3 Fully describe the harmonic interval between the violins and the flute at the beginning of bar 56.

[2 marks]

25.4 How many different chords are used in bars 62–64 inclusive?

[1 mark]

25.5 What cadence is heard from bar 67 beat 2 to bar 67 beat 3?

[1 mark]

25.6 What textural device is used between the flute and first violin from bar 69?

[1 mark]

25.7 Describe the use of harmony, texture and melody in the excerpt, showing how they relate to the rest of the movement.

[10 marks]

Total: 17 marks

Question 26

Track 26 The operas of Mozart

This excerpt is from a Mozart opera. Answer the following questions, which are based on the score excerpt printed below.

26.1 What is the tonality of the excerpt?

[1 mark]

26.2 Name a bar in which a first inversion tonic chord can be heard.

[1 mark]

26.3 Fully describe the chord on the first beat of bar 11.

[2 marks]

26.4 What cadence is heard from bar 11 beat 2 to bar 12 beat 1?

[1 mark]

26.5 At the start of which bar does the music reach the dominant key?

[1 mark]

26.6 What is the texture in the excerpt?

[1 mark]

26.7 Describe the use of rhythm, metre, harmony and melody in the excerpt, showing how they help Mozart to capture the emotions of Cherubino.

A translation of the excerpt is given below.

Italian

1 Non so piu cosa son cosa faccio
2 Or di foco ora sono di ghiaccio
3 Ogni donna cangiar di colore
4 Ogni donna mi fa paipitar
5 Solo ai nomi d'amor di diletto
6 Mi si turba mi salter ail petto

English

1 Is it pain is it pleasure that fills me
2 And with feverish ecstasy thrills me
3 At the sight of a woman I tremble
4 And my heart seems to burst into flame
5 Love! That word sets me hoping and fearing
6 Love! That word that I always am hearing

[10 marks]

Total: 17 marks

AS Level additional dictation questions

The following questions will give you further practice in completing the type of music dictation exercise given in Section A, question 3.

The excerpts are on tracks 27, 28 and 29

Question A

Track 27

Complete the melody in the bracketed sections of this aria by Mozart.

The rhythm is given above the stave.

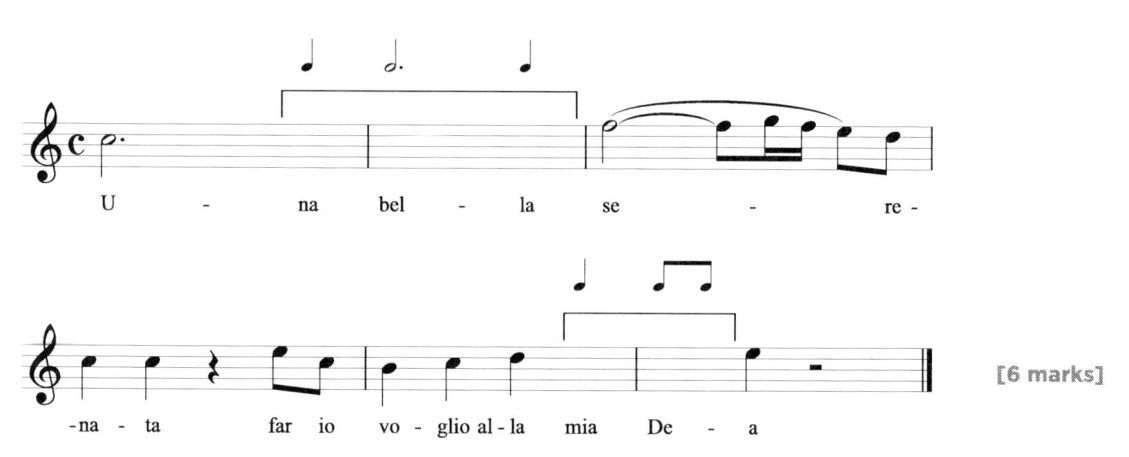

[6 marks]

Question B

Track 28

Complete the melody in the bracketed sections of this duet by Mozart.

The rhythm is given above the stave.

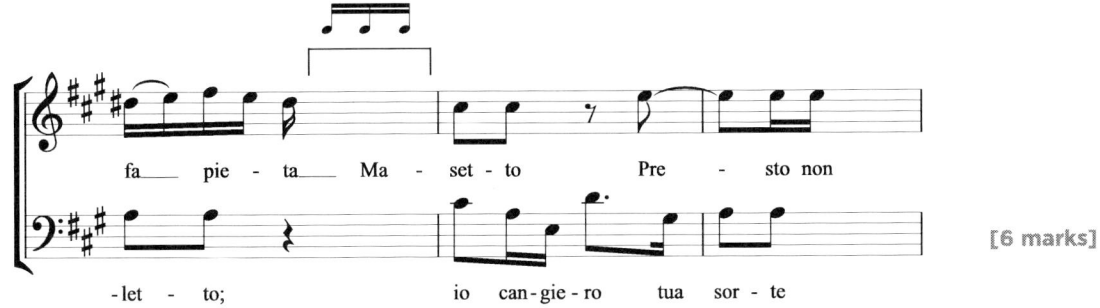

[6 marks]

Question C

Track 29

Complete the oboe melody in the bracketed sections of this oboe concerto by Handel.

The rhythm is given above the stave.

[6 marks]

AS Level additional Section B questions

The following questions will give you further practice in answering the type of question given in Section B, questions 25 and 26. In the exam you will be asked to answer **ONE** question of questions 25 and 26.

Section B: Analysis

25 minutes – 17 marks

The music for additional question 25 is on track 30
The music for additional question 26 is on track 31

Score excerpts are provided.

Additional question 25

Track 30 Baroque solo concerto

This excerpt is from a Purcell solo sonata. Answer the following questions, which are based on the score excerpt printed below.

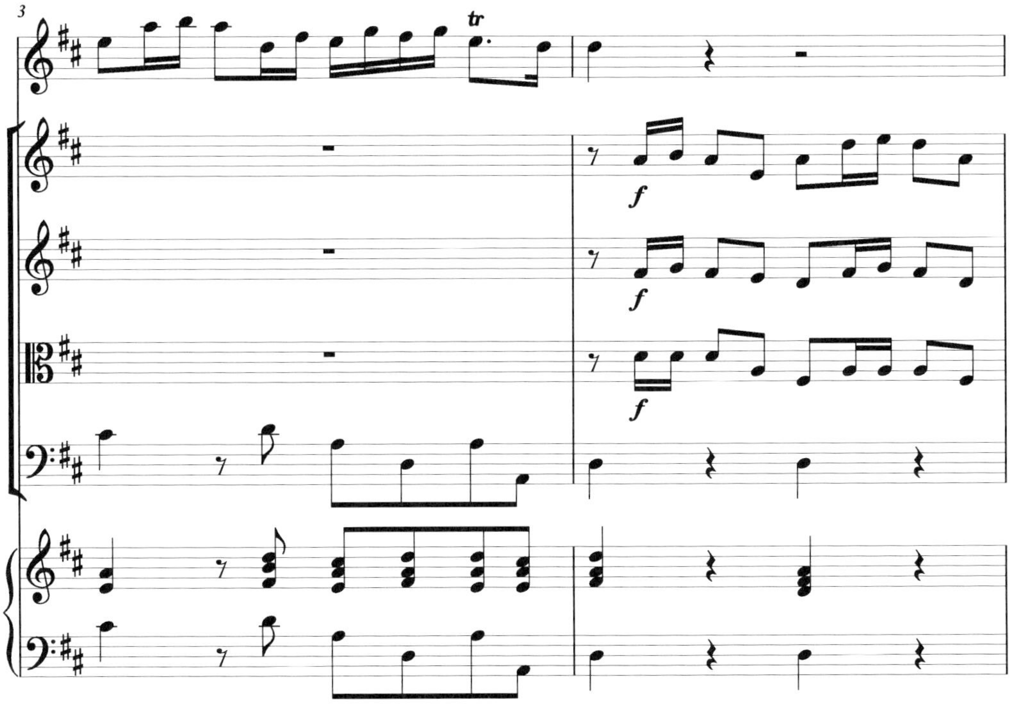
3
tr
f
f
f

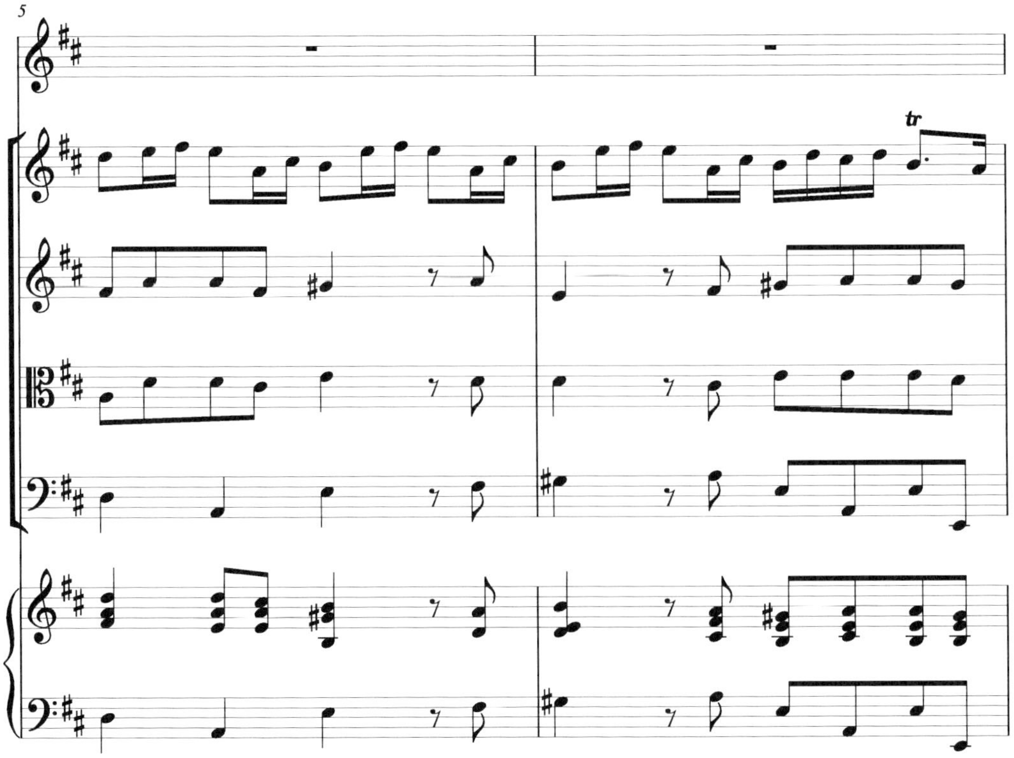
5
tr

AS LEVEL TESTS

AS/A LEVEL MUSIC LISTENING TESTS

25.1 Where is a chord other than the tonic first heard?

[1 mark]

25.2 Fully describe the second semiquaver in the melody.

[1 mark]

25.3 What is the key at the beginning of bar 8?

[1 mark]

25.4 Describe the texture employed in bars 7–9.

[1 mark]

25.5 Fully describe the type of dissonance heard on the start of the final beat of bar 13.

[2 marks]

25.6 What type of note is the final semiquaver of bar 13?

[1 mark]

25.7 Describe the use of melody, rhythm and texture in the excerpt, discussing the extent to which the composer was constrained by his choice of instrument.

[10 marks]

Total: 17 marks

Additional question 26

Track 31 The operas of Mozart

This excerpt is from an opera by Mozart. Answer the following questions, which are based on the score excerpt printed below.

Figaro

I thank your lord-ship kind-ly!
Bra - vo, Si-gnor pa - dro - ne!

Now I'm be-gin-ning to un-der-stand all this mys-ter-y, and to ap-
O - ra inco-min-cio a ca-pir il mi - ste - ro, e a ve - der

-pre-ciate your most gen - er - ous in - ten-tions.
schiet - to tut - to il vo - stro pro - get - to.

The king ap-points you am - bas - sa - dor in
A Lon - dra, è ve - ro? voi mi -

Lon - don, I go as cour - ier, and my Su -
- ni - stro, io cor - rie - ro, e la Su -

AS LEVEL TESTS

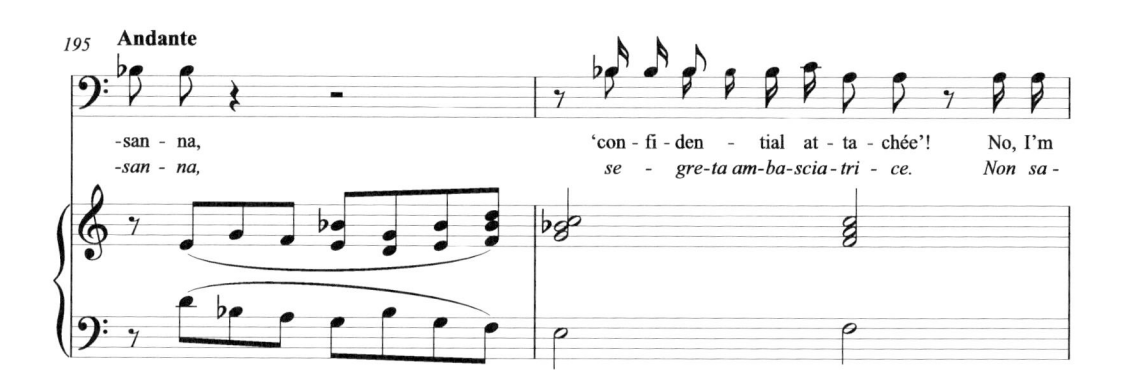

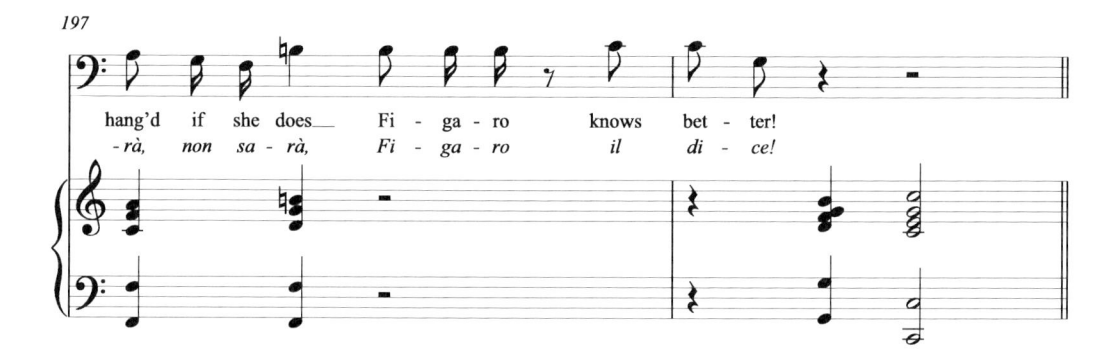

No.3 Cavatina

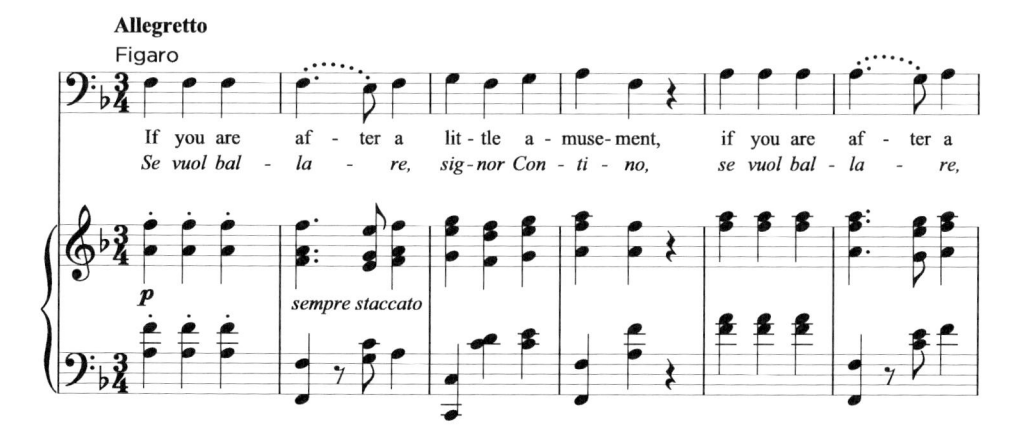

AS/A LEVEL MUSIC LISTENING TESTS

26.1 Give a location of a first inversion dominant 7th chord.

_____ [1 mark]

26.2 Describe the chord on which the aria begins.

_____ [1 mark]

26.3 Give **TWO** differences between the following melodic intervals.

Penultimate bar of the recitative:

final semiquaver of first beat and crotchet on the second beat

Final bar of the recitative:

first and second quavers

_____

_____ [2 marks]

26.4 Give a location of a cadential 6/4 progression.

_____ [1 mark]

26.5 Give a location of a second inversion chord **NOT** in a cadential progression.

_____ [1 mark]

26.6 What key is the aria in?

_____ [1 mark]

26.7 Explain how Mozart's handling of tempo, harmony, melody and metre helps to express Figaro's emotions in this recitative and aria, putting it into the context of what has just happened in the recitative.

A translation of the excerpt is given below.

Italian	English
recitative	*recitative*
1 Bravo, Signor padrone!	1 I thank your lordship kindly
2 Ora incomincio a capir il mistero,	2 Now I'm beginning to understand all this mystery
3 E a veder schietto tutto il vostro progetto	3 And to appreciate your most generous intentions
4 A Londra è vero?	4 The king appoints you
5 Voi ministro	5 Ambassador in London
6 Io corriero e la Susanna	6 I go as courier and my Susanna
7 Segreta ambasciatrice	7 Confidential attachée
8 Non sarà non sarà Figaro il dice!	8 No, I'm hang'd if she does. Figaro knows best!
aria	*aria*
9 Se vuol ballare signor Contino	9 If you are after a little amusement
10 Se vuol ballare signor Contino	10 If you are after a little amusement
11 Il chitarrino le suonerò	11 You may go dancing but I'll play the tune

[10 marks]

Total: 17 marks

A Level tests

A Level full paper

Section A: Listening

65 minutes – 56 marks

Answer **ALL THREE** questions in Area of Study 1 and **ALL THREE** questions in **TWO** other Areas of Study 2 to 7.

Area of Study 1: Western Classical tradition 1650–1910

Spend 25 minutes on this section.

Question 1 is on the excerpt of music on track 32
Question 2 is on the excerpt of music on track 33
Question 3 is on the excerpt of music on track 34

Question 1

Track 32

This excerpt is from Grieg's *Wedding day at Troldhaugen*.

1.1 Name the harmonic interval repeated throughout the first bar of the excerpt.

[1 mark]

1.2 Give **TWO** differences between the theme as it is first heard and the same theme when it returns.

[2 marks]

1.3 Which key has the piece modulated to by the end of the excerpt? Underline your answer.

    dominant   relative minor

    flattened leading note major   mediant major   [1 mark]

Total: 4 marks

Question 2

Track 33

Complete the melody in the bracketed sections of this excerpt from an oboe concerto by Handel.

The rhythm is given above the stave.

Total: 6 marks

Question 3

Track 34

The music is from an opera by Mozart.

Analyse the musical features that are typical of a Mozart opera.

Total: 10 marks

A LEVEL TESTS

Answer **ALL THREE** questions for **TWO** Areas of Study 2 to 7.

Area of Study 2: Pop music

Spend 20 minutes on this section

Question 4 is on the excerpt of music on track 35

Question 5 is on the excerpt of music on track 36

Question 6 is on the excerpt of music on track 37

Question 4

Track 35

This excerpt is from Joni Mitchell's 'California'. The lyrics are below.

1 California
2 Oh California I'm coming home
3 Oh make me feel good rock 'n' roll band
4 I'm your biggest fan
5 California I'm coming home
6 Oh it gets so lonely
7 When you're walking
8 And the streets are full of strangers
9 All the news of home you read
10 Just give you the blues
11 Just give you the blues

4.1 What is the interval heard in the vocal line between the two underlined syllables in line 2?

[1 mark]

4.2 What cadence is heard before line 6 (0:16–0:20)?

[1 mark]

4.3 How many different chords are used between lines 6 and 10?

[1 mark]

4.4 Starting from line 6, what effect is heard in the additional (pedal steel) guitar part? Underline your answer.

strumming   **harmonics**   **glissando**   **wah-wah**   [1 mark]

Total: 4 marks

AS/A LEVEL MUSIC LISTENING TESTS

Question 5

Track 36

This excerpt is from 'Let the sun shine' by Labrinth.

5.1 Identify the correct rhythm of the synth part that accompanies the vocal, which is repeated throughout the excerpt. Tick your answer.

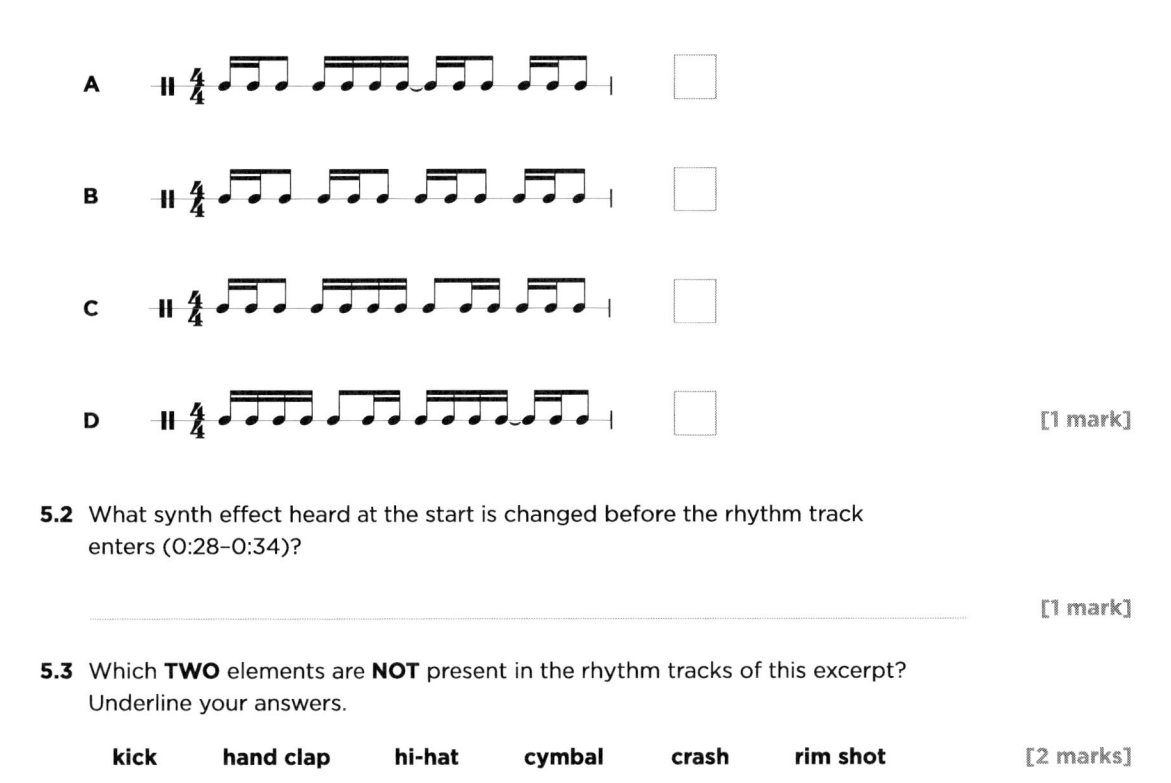

A

B

C

D

[1 mark]

5.2 What synth effect heard at the start is changed before the rhythm track enters (0:28–0:34)?

_____

[1 mark]

5.3 Which **TWO** elements are **NOT** present in the rhythm tracks of this excerpt? Underline your answers.

kick   **hand clap**   **hi-hat**   **cymbal**   **crash**   **rim shot**   [2 marks]

Total: 4 marks

Question 6

Track 37

This excerpt is from 'Master Blaster (Jammin')' by Stevie Wonder. The song shows strong influences of reggae, in particular of the music of Bob Marley.

Explain how Stevie Wonder uses musical elements to fuse his own style with aspects borrowed from the reggae style.

Total: 10 marks

Area of Study 3: Music for media

Spend 20 minutes on this section

Question 7 is on the excerpt of music on track 38
Question 8 is on the excerpt of music on track 39
Question 9 is on the excerpt of music on track 40

Question 7

Track 38

The excerpt is from Hans Zimmer's music for the film *Backdraft*. The cue is called 'Brothers'.

7.1 Give a suitable time signature for this cue.

[1 mark]

7.2 What harmonic device is heard from 0:12–0:22?

[1 mark]

7.3 What type of cadence is heard from 0:26–0:31?

[1 mark]

7.4 In which inversion is the final chord?

[1 mark]

Total: 4 marks

A LEVEL TESTS

Question 8

Track 39

The excerpt is from Michael Giacchino's music for season 4 of *Lost*. The cue is called 'C4-titude'.

8.1 Identify the correct shape for the top notes of the opening four chords.
Tick your answer.

A

B

C

D
[1 mark]

8.2 Which of the following features is **NOT** heard in this excerpt? Underline your answer.

ostinato   **sting**   **added-note harmonies**   **sequence**   [1 mark]

8.3 Name **TWO** string playing techniques heard in this excerpt.

_____

_____ [2 marks]

Total: 4 marks

Question 9

Track 40

The excerpt is from Bernard Herrmann's music for the science fiction film *The day the earth stood still* (1951). The cue is called 'Gort – the visor'.

Just after an alien flying saucer lands on earth, a peaceful alien ambassador is accidentally shot by US troops. The film cuts to his invincible robotic bodyguard exactly as this cue starts. After walking towards the body of its wounded comrade, the robot unleashes three ray-blasts from its visor (0:55, 1:01 and 1:07), destroying the soldiers' rifles with the first two and a tank with the third.

Explain how Herrmann uses musical elements to underscore this scene.

Total: 10 marks

Area of Study 4: Music for theatre

Spend 20 minutes on this section

Question 10 is on the excerpt of music on track 41
Question 11 is on the excerpt of music on track 42
Question 12 is on the excerpt of music on track 43

Question 10

Track 41

The excerpt is from Jason Robert Brown's musical *The last five years*. The song is called 'See, I'm smiling'.

10.1 On which degree of the scale does the melody begin?

[1 mark]

10.2 Which of the following represents the bass riff heard in the excerpt?

A
B
C
D

[1 mark]

10.3 At the opening of the excerpt, what is the repeated harmonic interval in the piano?

[1 mark]

10.4 Describe the chord heard at the end of the excerpt.

[1 mark]

Total: 4 marks

Question 11

Track 42

The excerpt is from Rodgers and Hammerstein's musical *South Pacific*. The song is called 'Some enchanted evening'. The lyrics for the excerpt are below.

1 Some enchanted evening
2 You may see a stranger
3 You may see a stranger
4 Across a crowded room
5 And somehow you know
6 You know even then
7 That somewhere you'll see her again and again

11.1 Which of the following harmonic features can be heard on the lyric 'even' (in line 6, underlined above)? Underline your answer.

   pedal   **false relation**   **suspension**   **tierce de picardie**   [1 mark]

11.2 Which type of chord is heard at the lyric 'across a' (in line 4, underlined above)? Underline your answer.

   major 7th   **augmented**   **diminished**   **minor 7th**   [1 mark]

11.3 The lyric 'You may see a stranger' is heard twice in the excerpt. The melody for the first time is written below.

On the stave below, write out the melody when the words are heard for the second time.

[2 marks]

Total: 4 marks

Question 12

Track 43

The excerpt is from Schönberg and Boublil's musical *Miss Saigon*. The song is called 'Why, God, why?' The lyrics are below.

The musical is set during the Vietnam war in the 1970s. The character singing is the US Marine, Chris, who has met the seventeen-year-old girl Kim in Vietnam shortly before he is due to leave the country.

1   Why does Saigon never sleep at night?
2   Why does this girl smell of orange trees?
3   How can I feel good when nothing's right?
4   Why is she cool when there is no breeze?
5   Vietnam
6   You don't give answers, do you friend?
7   Just questions that don't ever end

Explain how the composer's use of musical elements conveys Chris's feelings.

Total: 10 marks

Area of Study 5: Jazz

Spend 20 minutes on this section

Question 13 is on the excerpt of music on track 44

Question 14 is on the excerpt of music on track 45

Question 15 is on the excerpt of music on track 46

Question 13

Track 44

The excerpt is from the Impossible Gentlemen's album *Internationally recognised aliens*. The track is called 'Barber blues'.

13.1 What is the texture at the beginning of the excerpt?

[1 mark]

13.2 Which rhythm accurately notates the rhythm of the opening two bars?
Tick your answer.

[1 mark]

13.3 When the band enters, what device does the pianist use to extend the melody?

[1 mark]

13.4 At 0:30, on what degree of the scale does the melody begin? Underline your answer.

tonic   mediant   subdominant   dominant

[1 mark]

Total: 4 marks

A LEVEL TESTS

Question 14

Track 45

The excerpt is from Duke Ellington's track 'In a sentimental mood'.

14.1 The opening of the melody at 0:07 is shown below. Circle the incorrect note.

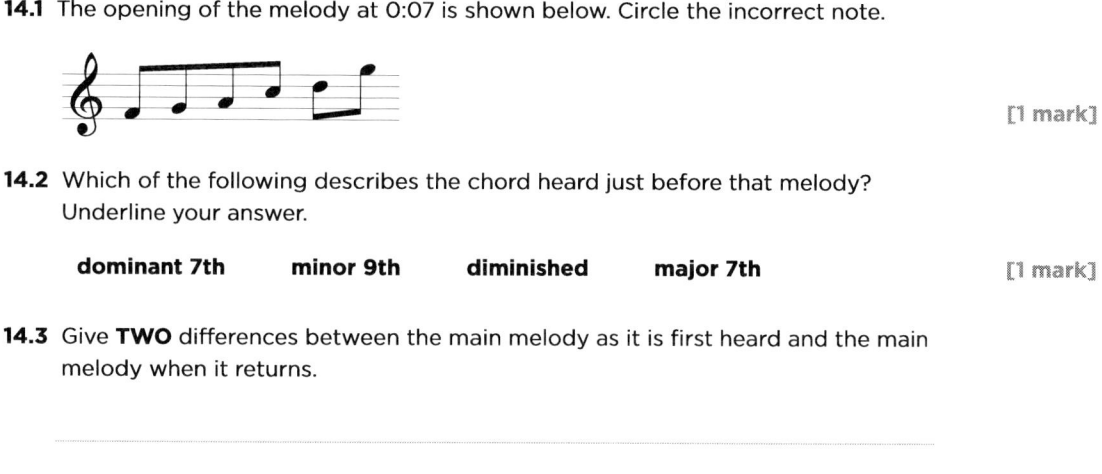

[1 mark]

14.2 Which of the following describes the chord heard just before that melody? Underline your answer.

dominant 7th **minor 9th** **diminished** **major 7th**

[1 mark]

14.3 Give **TWO** differences between the main melody as it is first heard and the main melody when it returns.

_____

_____

[2 marks]

Total: 4 marks

Question 15

Track 46

The excerpt is from the track 'Summertime' from Miles Davis's album *Porgy and Bess*.

Explain how Mile Davis's use of the musical features brings his own style to this jazz standard.

Total: 10 marks

Area of Study 6: Contemporary traditional music

Spend 20 minutes on this section

Question 16 is on the excerpt of music on track 47
Question 17 is on the excerpt of music on track 48
Question 18 is on the excerpt of music on track 49

Question 16

Track 47

The excerpt is from Ali Farka Touré and Toumani Diabaté's track 'Ruby' from their album *Ali and Toumani*.

16.1 Apart from bass, name **ONE** of the two other instruments.

[1 mark]

16.2 Give a suitable time signature for this excerpt.

[1 mark]

16.3 Apart from the tonic, what other degree of the scale is heard in the bass?

[1 mark]

16.4 Which **ONE** of the following is **NOT** a feature of this excerpt? Underline your answer.

    improvisation   **ostinato**   **modulation**   **cross-rhythms**   [1 mark]

Total: 4 marks

Question 17

Track 48

The excerpt is from the track 'Adios Nonino', played by Astor Piazzolla in a quintet.

17.1 What is the tonality at the beginning of the excerpt?

[1 mark]

17.2 What is the tonality at the end of the excerpt?

[1 mark]

17.3 Name **TWO** stringed instruments you can hear playing.

[2 marks]

Total: 4 marks

Question 18

Track 49

The excerpt is from Bellowhead's track 'A-begging I will go' from the album *Hedonism*. The track is Bellowhead's arrangement of a traditional English folksong. The lyrics for the excerpt are below.

1 Of all the trades in England, the begging is the best
2 For when a beggar's tired, he can lay him down to rest

3 And a-begging I will go, and a-begging I will go

4 I've a pocket for my oatmeal and another for my salt
5 And with my leg and crutches you should see how I can bolt

6 And a-begging I will go, and a-begging I will go

7 There's patches on my coat, and on my right eye too
8 When it comes to pretty girls, I can see as well as you

9 And a-begging I will go, and a-begging I will go
10 A-begging I will go, and a-begging I will go

Describe how Bellowhead make use of musical elements to blend traditional musical features with more modern ones.

Total: 10 marks

Area of Study 7: Art music since 1910

Spend 20 minutes on this section

Question 19 is on the excerpt of music on track 50

Question 20 is on the excerpt of music on track 51

Question 21 is on the excerpt of music on track 52

Question 19

Track 50

The excerpt is from *Four organs* by Steve Reich.

19.1 How many beats in a bar are there in the excerpt?

_____

[1 mark]

19.2 Which of the following sets of three notes is heard before the chord enters each time?

A

B

C

D

[1 mark]

19.3 What happens to the texture on the third of these notes at the end of the excerpt?

_____

[1 mark]

19.4 Besides the organ, which instrument can be heard throughout the excerpt?

_____

[1 mark]

Total: 4 marks

Question 20

Track 51

The excerpt is from the 'Little polka' movement of Stravinsky's *Jazz suite 2*.

20.1 Which **TWO** of the following instruments have solos during the excerpt?
Underline your answers.

xylophone   **alto saxophone**   **glockenspiel**

trumpet   **clarinet**   [2 marks]

20.2 What is the tonality of the excerpt?

_____

[1 mark]

20.3 Which of the following patterns describes the bass part in the opening two bars?
Underline your answer.

I – IV – I – IV   I – V – I – V   IV – I – IV – I   V – I – V – I   [1 mark]

Total: 4 marks

Question 21

Track 52

The excerpt is from James Macmillan's *Birthday present*.

Explain how the use of musical elements in the excerpt brings a new meaning to a popular tune.

Total: 10 marks

Section B: Analysis

40 minutes – 34 marks

Answer **two** questions from Questions 22–24.

The music for question 22 is on track 53

The music for question 23 is on track 54

The music for question 24 is on track 55

Score excerpts are provided.

Question 22

Track 53 – Baroque solo concerto

The excerpt is from Vivaldi's Flute concerto in D major, third movement.

Answer the following questions, which are based on the score excerpt printed below.

A LEVEL TESTS

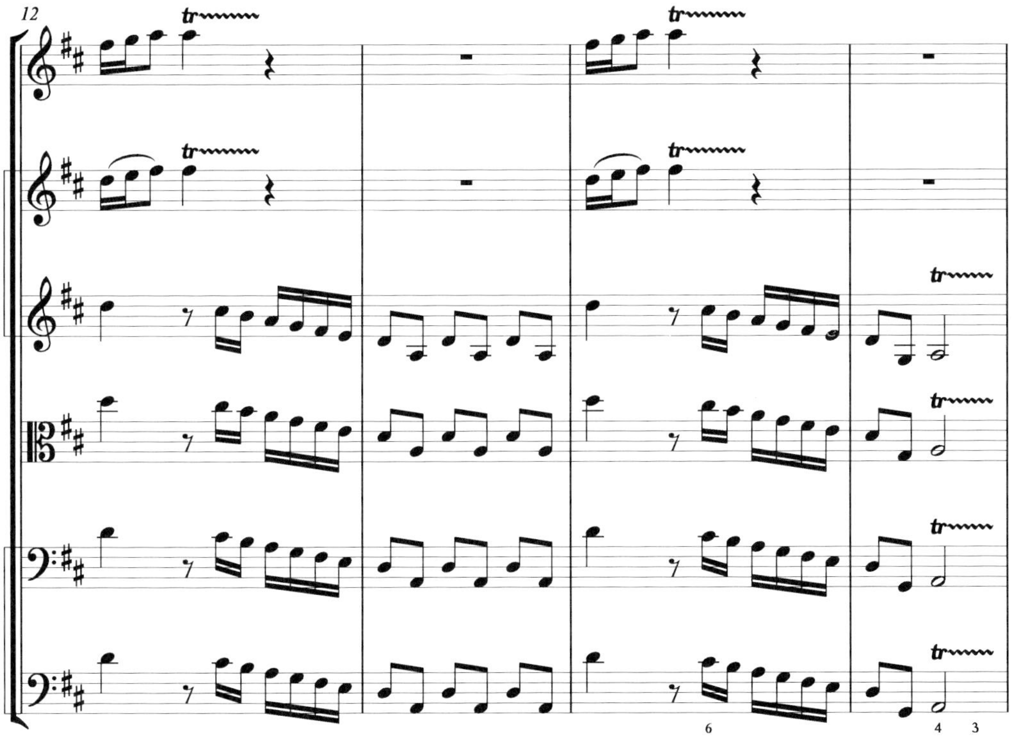
12
tr
6
4 3

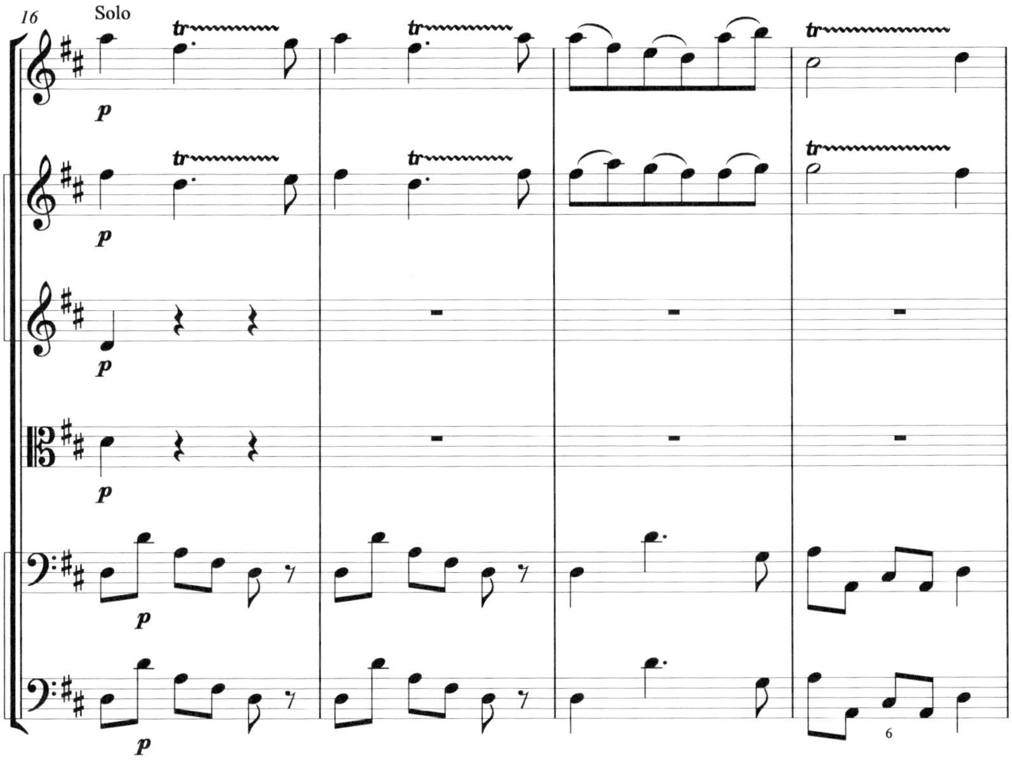
16
Solo
tr
p
6

22.1 What is the meaning of the '6' under the music at the beginning of bar 3?

[1 mark]

22.2 Give the full name of the harmonic interval between the cello and the viola on the first beat of bar 5.

[1 mark]

22.3 Analyse Vivaldi's approach to texture in the excerpt, discussing ways in which this is typical of his solo concertos.

[5 marks]

22.4 Analyse Vivaldi's approach to melody, rhythm and structure in the excerpt and explain how the excerpt relates to the third movement as a whole.

[10 marks]

Total: 17 marks

A LEVEL TESTS

Question 23

Track 54 – The operas of Mozart

The excerpt is from Mozart's *Le nozze di Figaro*, Act 1 no. 1.

Answer the following questions, which are based on the score excerpt printed below.

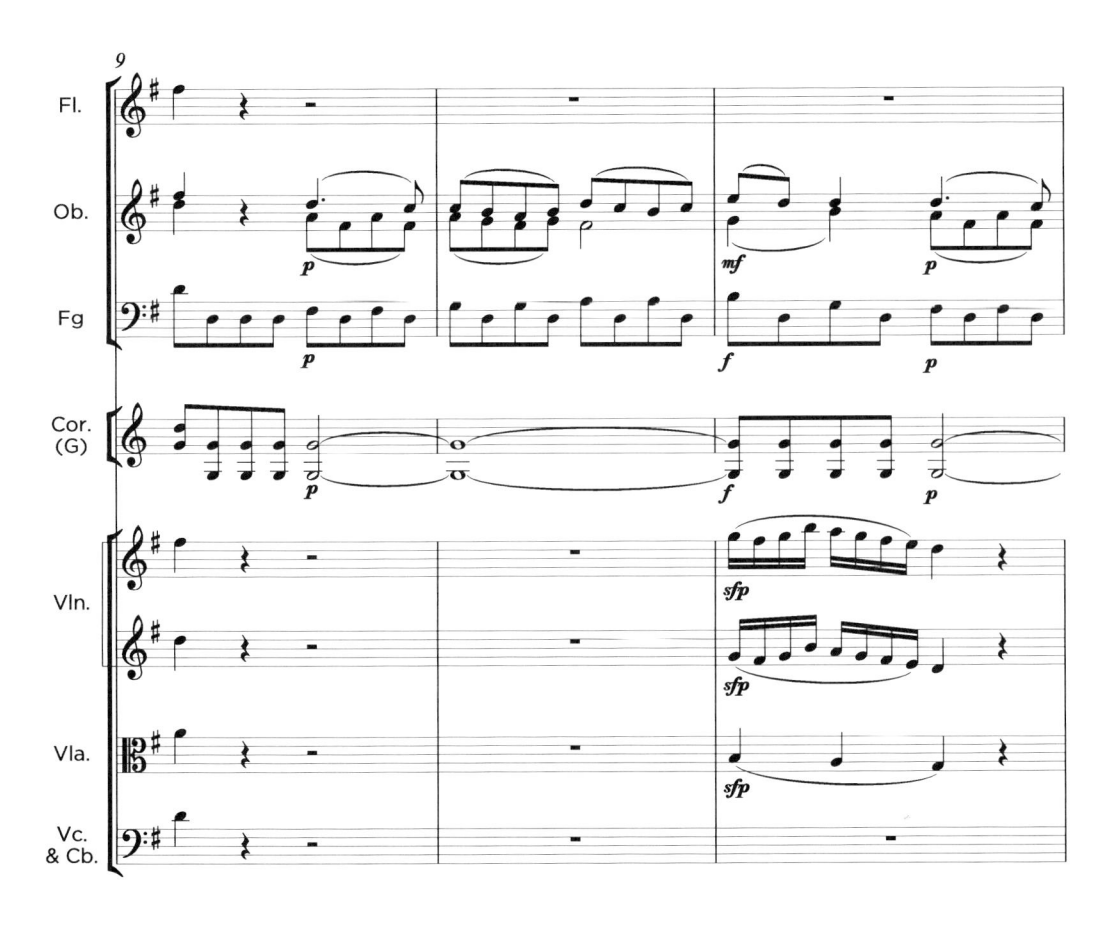

AS/A LEVEL MUSIC LISTENING TESTS

A LEVEL TESTS

18
Fl.
Ob.
Fg
Cor.
(G)
a 2
Fig.
FIGARO (misurando)
Cin - que...
Vln.
Vla.
Vc.
& Cb.

21
Fg
Fig.
die - ci...
Vln.
Vla.
Vc.
& Cb.

A LEVEL TESTS

AS/A LEVEL MUSIC LISTENING TESTS

A LEVEL TESTS

AS/A LEVEL MUSIC LISTENING TESTS

23.1 In concert pitch, which **TWO** degrees of the scale do the horns first play (at bar 6)?

_____
[1 mark]

23.2 Name the chord heard in bar 45.

_____
[1 mark]

23.3 Describe Mozart's use of the orchestra in this excerpt and discuss how this is typical of his writing.

_____

_____

_____

_____

_____

[5 marks]

AS/A LEVEL MUSIC LISTENING TESTS

23.4 Analyse the melody, texture and rhythm in this duet and explain how these aid the dramatic setting.

[10 marks]

Total: 17 marks

Question 24

Track 55 – 19th-century piano music

The excerpt is from Brahms's Intermezzo in A major op. 118 no. 2.

Answer the following questions, which are based on the score excerpt printed below.

AS/A LEVEL MUSIC LISTENING TESTS

24.1 Describe fully the chord on the first beat of bar 3.

_____ [1 mark]

24.2 Name the interval between the highest and lowest pitches heard on the first beat of bar 14.

_____ [1 mark]

24.3 Analyse Brahms's approach to rhythm in the melody during the excerpt, discussing ways in which this is typical of his style.

_____
_____
_____
_____
_____ [5 marks]

24.4 Describe Brahms's use of harmony, melody and texture in this piece and explain how they differ from what one might expect to hear in the music of Chopin or Grieg.

_____
_____
_____
_____
_____
_____
_____
_____
_____
_____ [10 marks]

Total: 17 marks

A Level additional dictation questions

The following questions will give you further practice in completing the type of music dictation exercise given in Section A, question 2.

Question A

Track 56

Complete the melody and bass in the bracketed sections of this violin concerto by Vivaldi.

The rhythm is given above the stave.

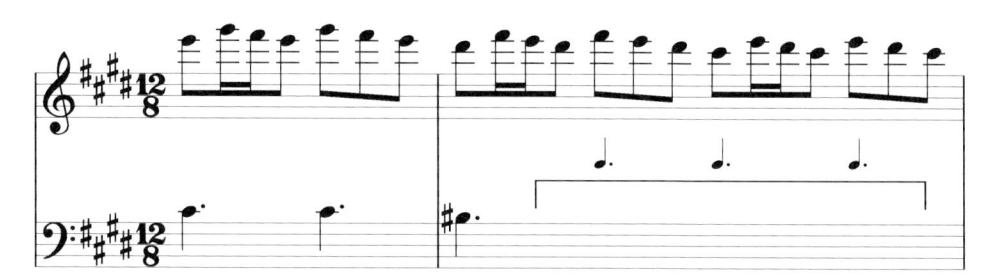

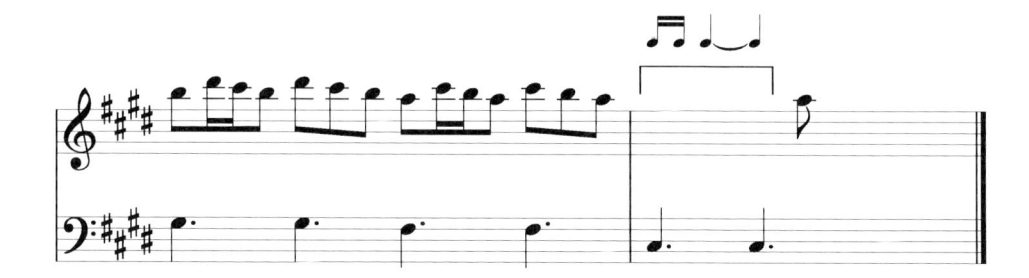

[6 marks]

AS/A LEVEL MUSIC LISTENING TESTS

Question B

Track 57

Complete the melody and bass in the bracketed sections of this piece by Chopin.

The rhythm is given above the stave.

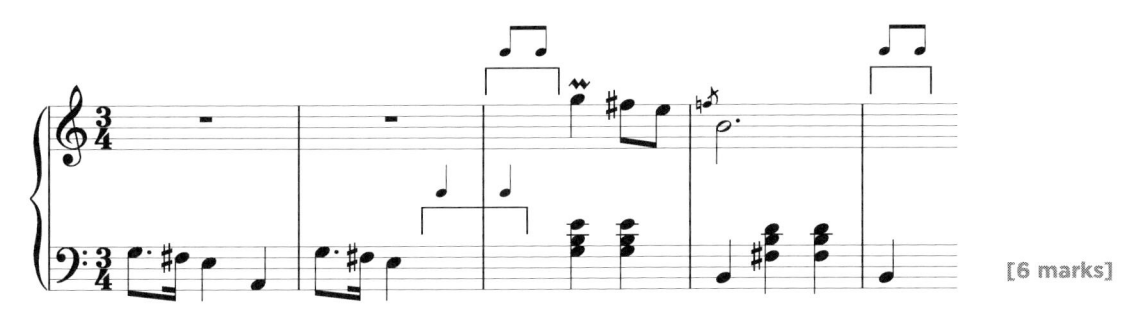

[6 marks]

Question C

Track 58

Complete the melody and bass in the bracketed sections of this aria by Mozart.

The rhythm is given above the stave.

wie noch kein Au-ge je ge-sehn! Ich fuel-'es ich

fuel-'es wie dies Goe-tter-bild

[6 marks]

A Level additional Section B questions

The following questions will give you further practice in answering the type of question given in Section B, questions 22-24. In the exam you will be asked to answer **TWO** questions from questions 22-24.

Section B: Analysis

40 minutes – 34 marks

Answer **TWO** questions from questions 22-24.

The music for additional question 22 is on track 59

The music for additional question 23 is on track 60

The music for additional question 24 is on track 61

Score excerpts are provided.

Additional question 22

Track 59 – Baroque solo concerto

The excerpt is from Bach's Violin concerto in A minor, third movement.

Answer the following questions, which are based on the score excerpt printed below.

AS/A LEVEL MUSIC LISTENING TESTS

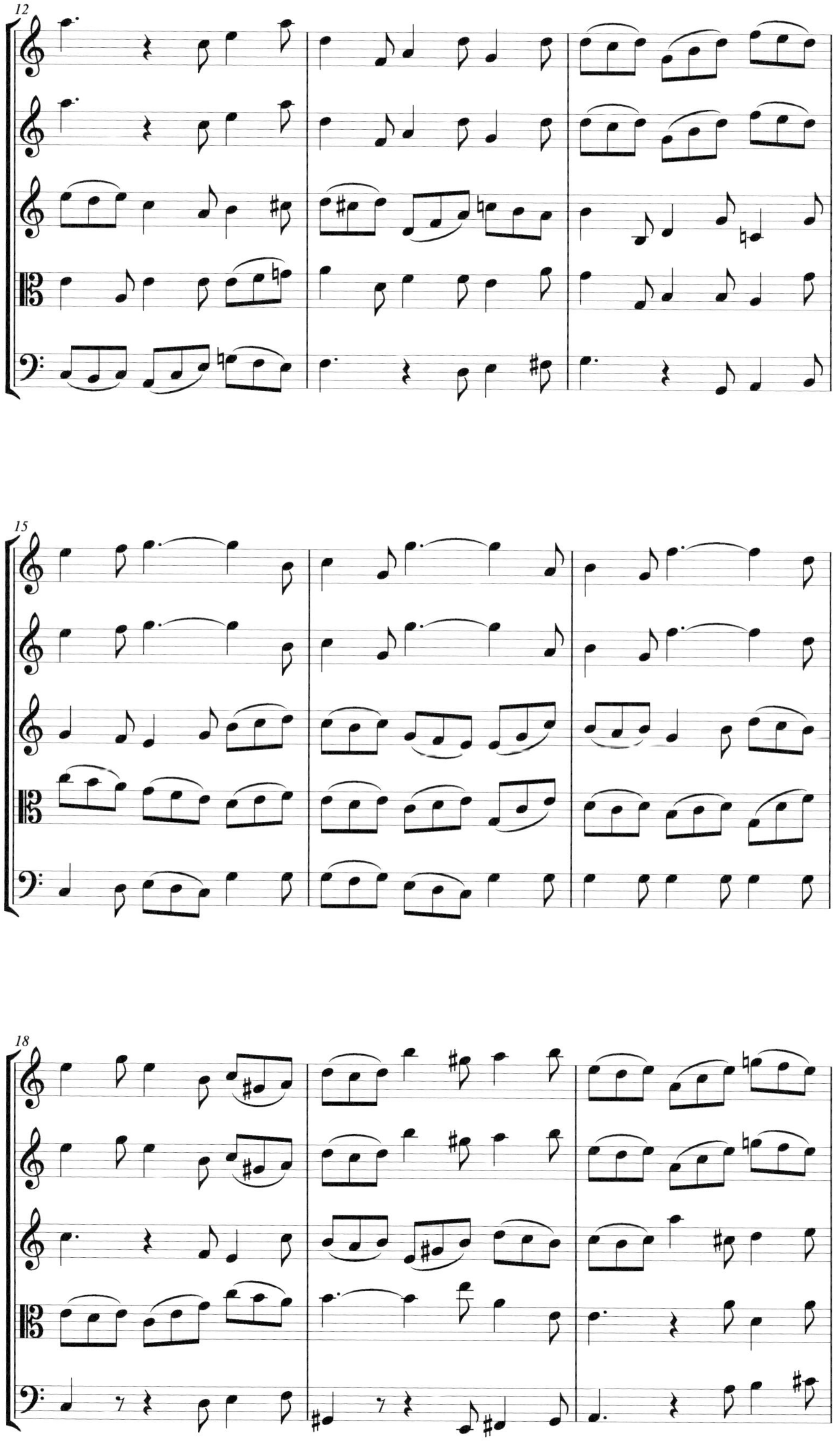
12
15
18

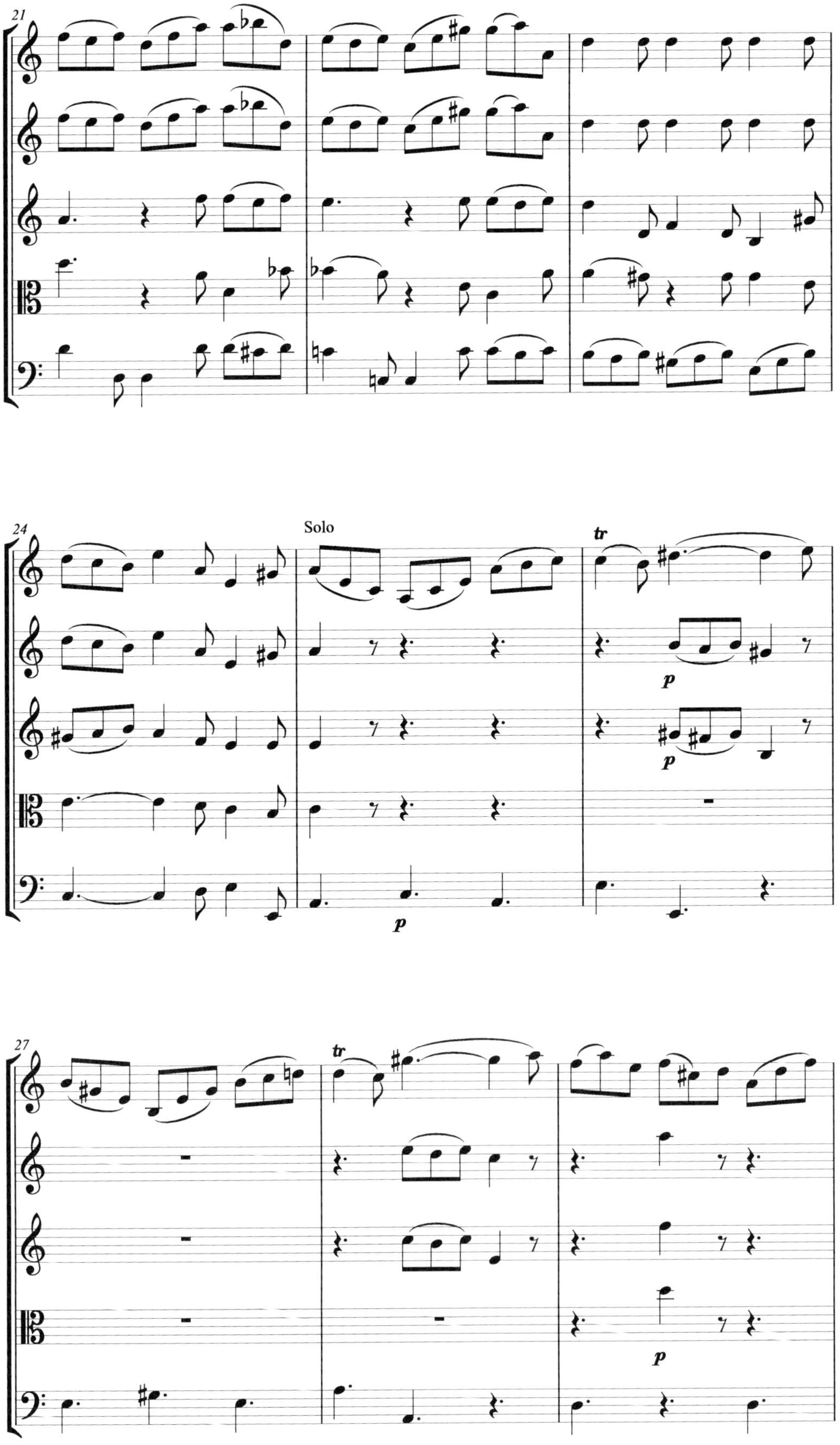
21
24
Solo
tr
p
27
tr
p

A LEVEL TESTS

AS/A LEVEL MUSIC LISTENING TESTS

22.1 What is the key at the beginning of bar 14?

[1 mark]

22.2 Fully describe the melodic device employed in bars 33–38.

[1 mark]

22.3 Analyse Bach's approach to dissonance in the excerpt, discussing ways in which this is typical of the baroque period.

[5 marks]

22.4 In terms of texture, melody and rhythm, discuss how Bach uses the solo instrument in this movement and explore how this relates to the approaches of other baroque composers.

[10 marks]

Total: 17 marks

Additional question 23

Track 60 – The operas of Mozart

The excerpt is from the Overture of Mozart's opera *Le nozze di Figaro*.

Answer the following questions, which are based on the score excerpt printed below.

A LEVEL TESTS

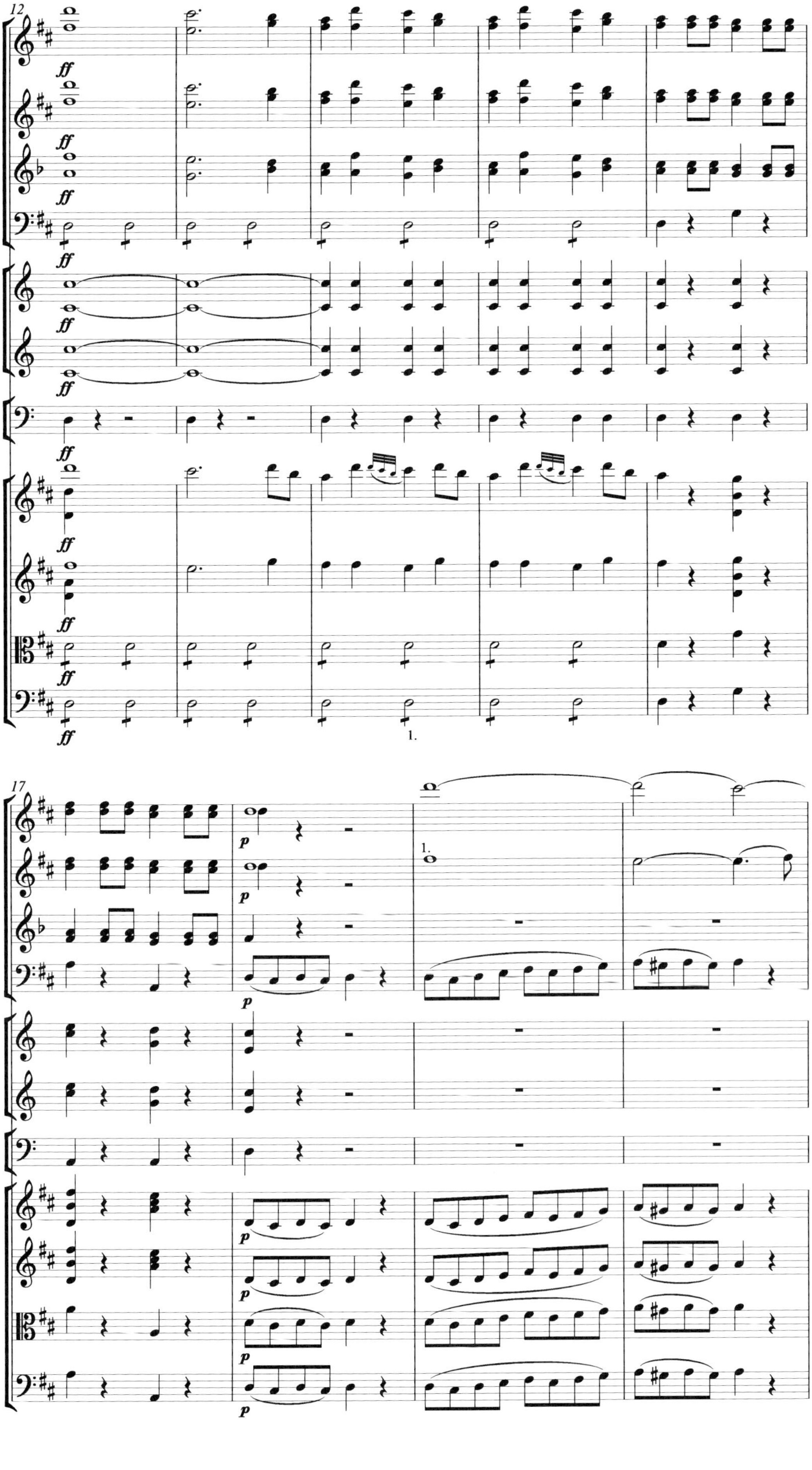
12
ff
1.
17
p
1.

A LEVEL TESTS

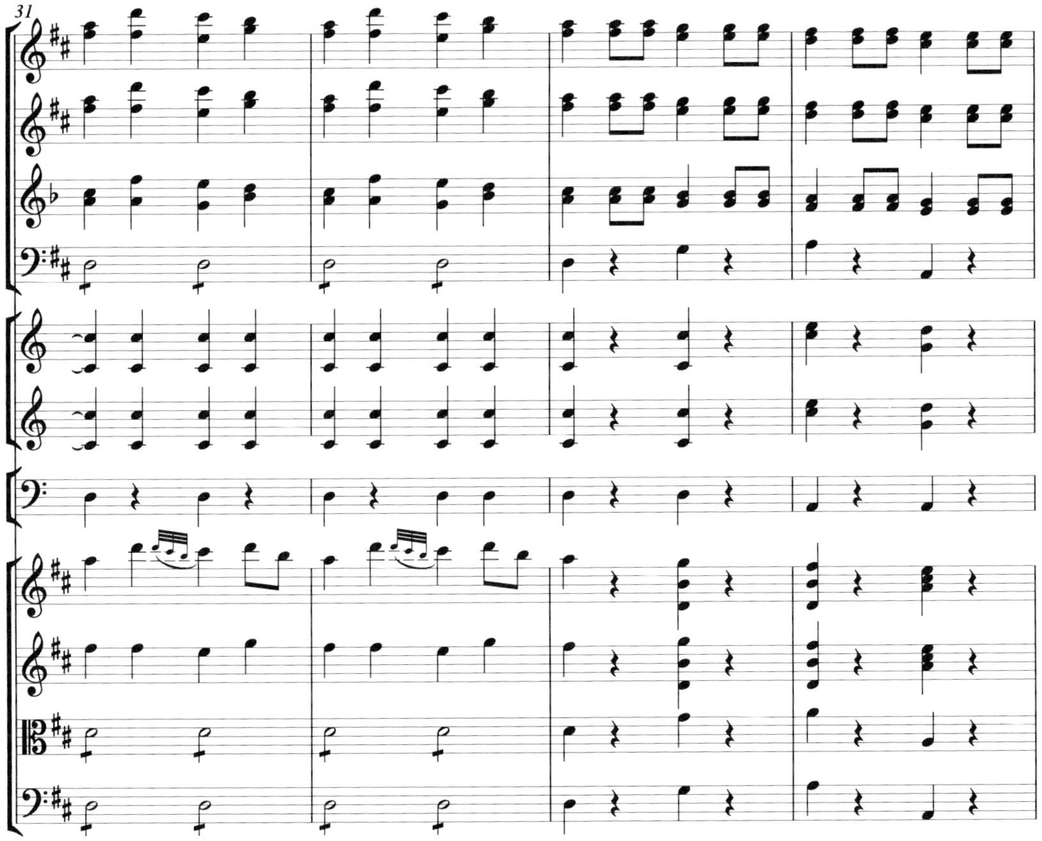
31

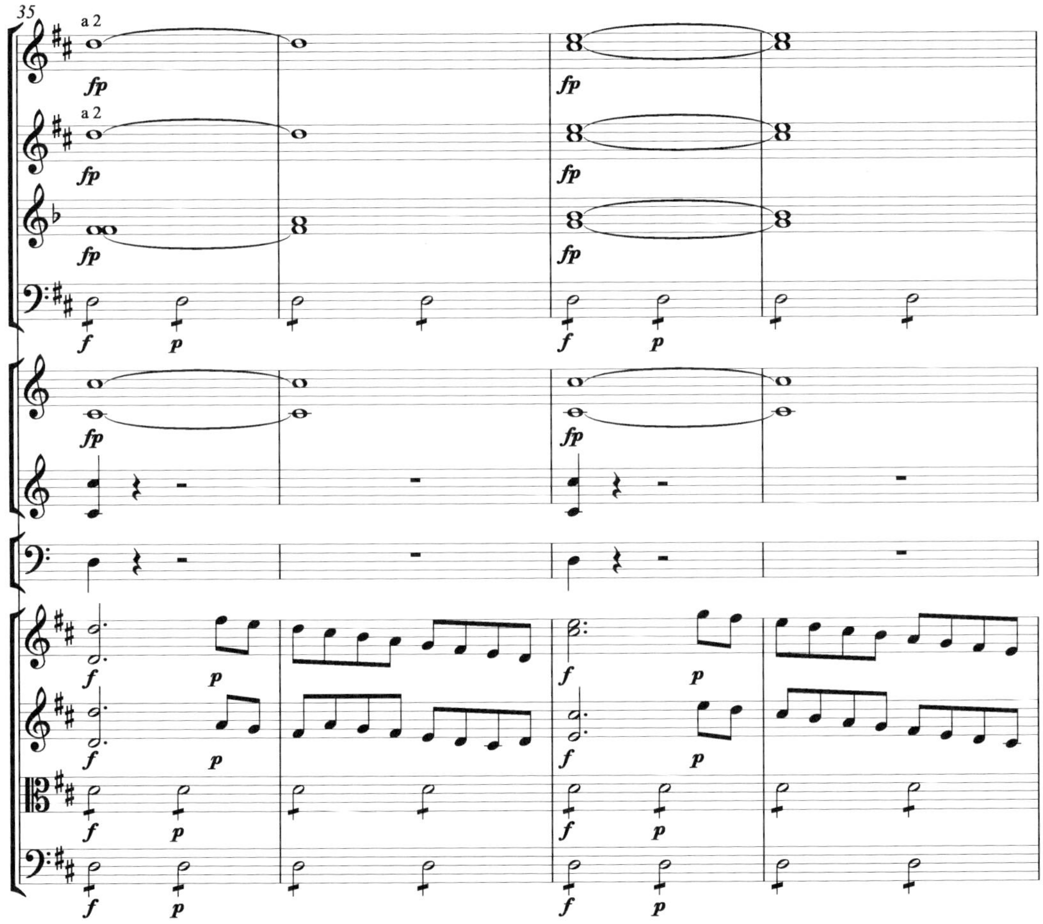
35
a 2
fp
f
p

A LEVEL TESTS

AS/A LEVEL MUSIC LISTENING TESTS

A LEVEL TESTS

23.1 Fully describe the cello part from bar 7 to the beginning of bar 16.

[1 mark]

23.2 What is the key at the end of the excerpt?

[1 mark]

23.3 Analyse Mozart's use of the orchestra in the excerpt, describing how this is typical of his style.

[5 marks]

23.4 Analyse Mozart's use of melody, harmony and texture in the excerpt, explaining how the excerpt – and the overture as a whole – provide a suitable introduction to the opera.

[10 marks]

Total: 17 marks

Additional question 24

Track 61 – 19th-century piano music

The excerpt is from Grieg's *Norwegian march* op. 54 no. 2.

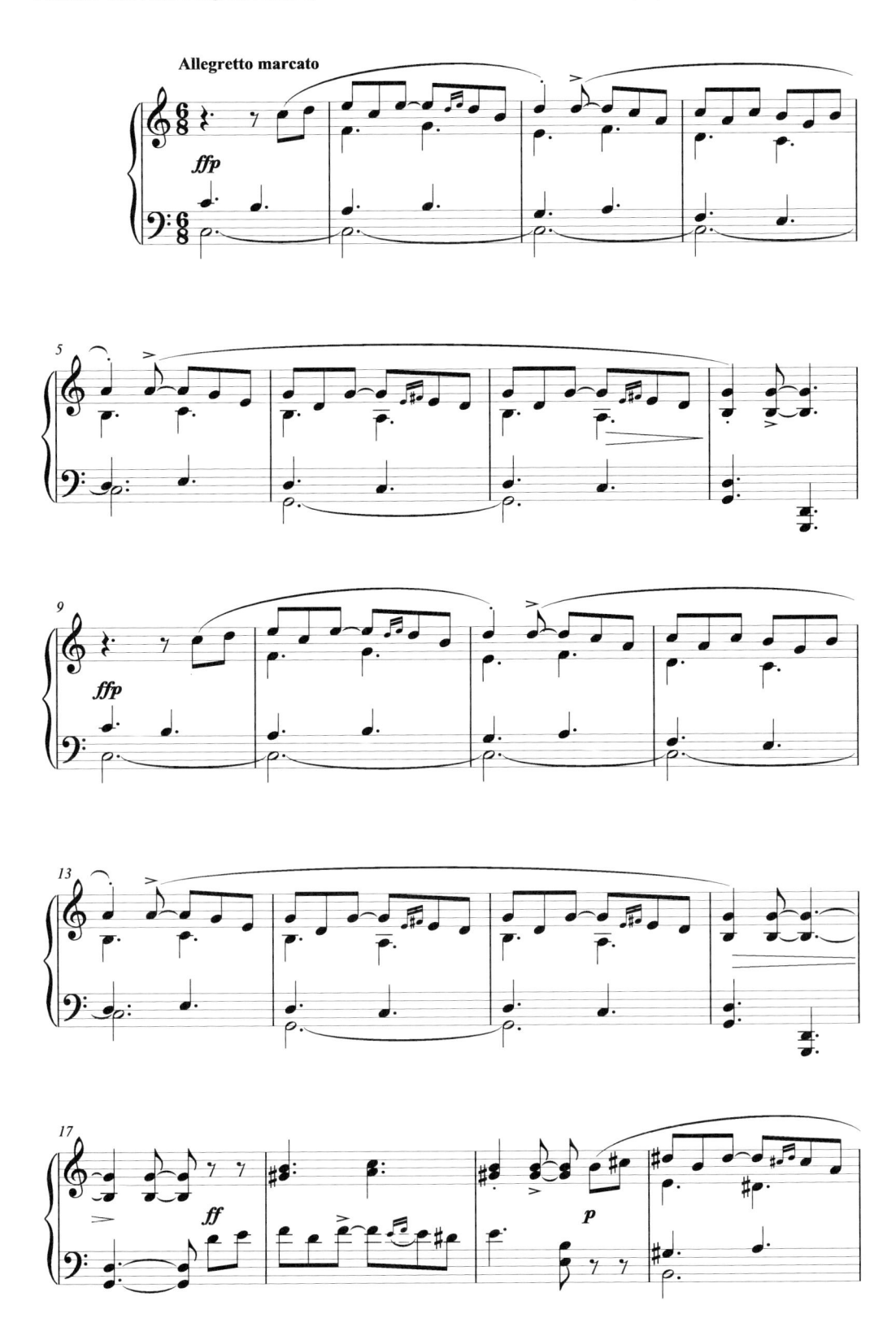

Answer the following questions, which are based on the score excerpt printed below.

A LEVEL TESTS

AS/A LEVEL MUSIC LISTENING TESTS

A LEVEL TESTS

24.1 Fully describe the chord played on beat 2 of bar 22, relating it to the tonic.

[1 mark]

24.2 What is the compass of the left-hand (bass) part in the excerpt?

[1 mark]

24.3 Analyse Grieg's approach to harmony in the excerpt, putting this in the context of his wider output.

[5 marks]

24.4 Analyse Grieg's use of melody, rhythm, structure and dynamics in the excerpt, and explain how these uses complement the rest of the movement.

[10 marks]

Total: 17 marks

Optional Areas of Study (AoS): additional questions

AREA OF STUDY 2:
Pop music

Question A

Track 62

The excerpt is from Joni Mitchell's 'The circle game'. The lyrics for the excerpt are below.

1   Yesterday a child came out to wonder
2   Caught a dragonfly inside a jar
3   Fearful when the sky was full of thunder
4   And tearful at the falling of a star

A.1 How many different bass notes are heard in the introduction before the voice enters?

[1 mark]

A.2 On what degree of the scale does the vocal line begin?

[1 mark]

A.3 To which chord does the music move in line 3?

[1 mark]

A.4 Which **TWO** of the following are **NOT** features of this excerpt? Underline your answers.

   chromaticism   tonic pedal   imperfect cadence

   plagal cadence   diatonic melody

[2 marks]

Total: 5 marks

OPTIONAL AREAS OF STUDY (AOS): ADDITIONAL QUESTIONS

Question B

Track 63

The excerpt is from 'Broken-hearted girl' by Beyoncé. The lyrics for the chorus (heard at the start of the excerpt) are below.

1. I don't wanna be without you, babe
2. I don't want a broken heart
3. Don't wanna take a breath without you, babe
4. I don't wanna play that part
5. I know that I love you, but let me just say
6. I don't wanna love you in no kind of way, no no
7. I don't want a broken heart
8. I don't wanna play the broken-hearted girl
9. No, no, no broken-hearted girl
10. I'm no broken-hearted girl

B.1 Complete the chord progression heard at the start of the chorus by writing in **TWO** chord names.

    Dm   B♭   _____   _____ [2 marks]

B.2 What is the compass of line 2?

[1 mark]

B.3 Identify the chord on the second 'no' (underlined) at the end of line 6.

[1 mark]

B.4 Name **ONE** instrument that is added during the course of this excerpt.

[1 mark]

Total: 5 marks

Question C

Track 64

The excerpt is from 'Lose yourself to dance' by Daft Punk. The lyrics for the excerpt are below.

CHORUS

1. Lose yourself to dance
2. Lose yourself to dance
3. Lose yourself to dance
4. Lose yourself to dance
5. Lose yourself to dance

VERSE

6. I know you don't get chance to take a break this often
7. I know your life is speeding and it isn't stopping
8. You take my shirt and just go ahead and wipe up all the
9. Sweat, sweat, sweat

[CHORUS]

AS/A LEVEL MUSIC LISTENING TESTS

C.1 Complete the melodic shape of the first line of the chorus by adding **TWO** accidentals to the outline shown below.

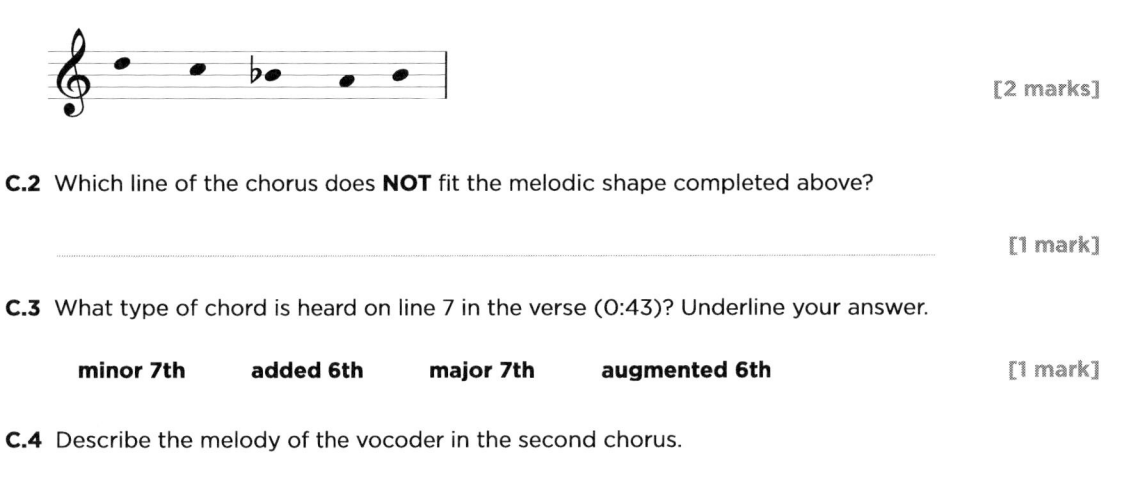

[2 marks]

C.2 Which line of the chorus does **NOT** fit the melodic shape completed above?

[1 mark]

C.3 What type of chord is heard on line 7 in the verse (0:43)? Underline your answer.

    minor 7th   **added 6th**   **major 7th**   **augmented 6th** [1 mark]

C.4 Describe the melody of the vocoder in the second chorus.

[1 mark]

Total: 5 marks

Question D

Track 65

The excerpt is from the radio edit of 'Earthquake' by Labrinth (feat. Tinie Tempah).

D.1 Early in the excerpt, what is the name of the effect used on the vocals on the words 'breaker' (0:04) and 'make-up' (0:11)? Underline your answer.

    reverb   **delay**   **auto-tune**   **panning** [1 mark]

D.2 What is the melodic interval heard on the word 'earthquake' (heard at 0:29 and 0:34)?

[1 mark]

D.3 Identify **TWO** effects that are used in the synth lead in this excerpt. Underline your answers.

    flanging   **portamento**   **wah-wah**   **tremolo**   **filtering** [2 marks]

D.4 What is the tonality of the excerpt?

[1 mark]

Total: 5 marks

AREA OF STUDY 3:
Music for media

Question A

Track 66

The excerpt is from Thomas Newman's score to the film *The Iron Lady*. The cue is called 'Exclusion zone'.

A.1 How many different pitches are heard in the bass melody at 0:06?

_____

[1 mark]

A.2 Name **TWO** orchestral instruments introduced during the course of the excerpt.

_____

_____

[2 marks]

A.3 What is the time signature at the start of the excerpt?

_____

[1 mark]

A.4 Which time signature is established by the end of the excerpt?

_____

[1 mark]

Total: 5 marks

AS/A LEVEL MUSIC LISTENING TESTS

Question B

Track 67

The excerpt is from Nobuo Uematsu's score for the video game *Blue Dragon*.
The track is called 'In search of the ruins'.

B.1 What is the opening melodic interval between the bass notes heard at the start of the track?

_____ [1 mark]

B.2 Identify the correct shape of the melody when it first appears. Tick your answer.

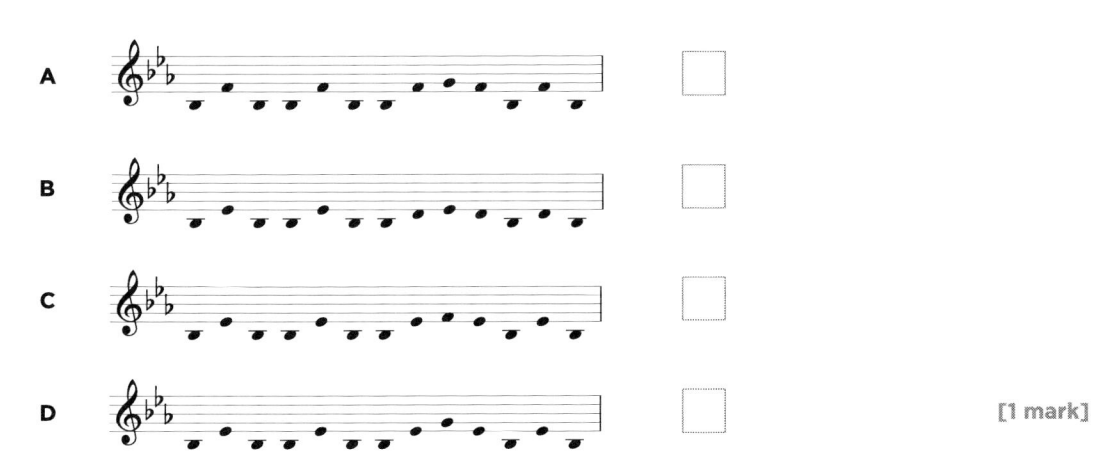

A

B

C

D

[1 mark]

B.3 Which **TWO** of the following are used to develop the melody in this excerpt? Underline your answers.

augmentation   **sequence**   **diminution**

fragmentation   **canon**

[2 marks]

B.4 Name the only non-synthesised instrument heard in this excerpt.

_____ [1 mark]

Total: 5 marks

OPTIONAL AREAS OF STUDY (AOS): ADDITIONAL QUESTIONS

Question C

Track 68

The excerpt is from Bernard Herrmann's score to the film *Marnie*. The cue is called 'The hotel room'.

C.1 Name **ONE** rhythmic feature that is consistently used in this excerpt.

[1 mark]

C.2 Name the playing technique used by the strings in this excerpt.

[1 mark]

C.3 Identify the **TWO** woodwind instruments that have solos from 0:16–0:28.

[2 marks]

C.4 Which of the following techniques is **NOT** used to develop the opening melodic fragment? Underline your answer.

fragmentation   **inversion**   **sequence**   **imitation**

[1 mark]

Total: 5 marks

Question D

Track 69

The excerpt is from Thomas Newman's score to the film *The Green Mile*. The cue is called 'Foolishment'.

D.1 Identify the solo instrument.

[1 mark]

D.2 What is the interval between the bass and the high string note heard at the end of the track (0:43)?

[1 mark]

D.3 Which **TWO** of the following are features of the excerpt? Underline your answers.

ostinato   **drone**   **tremolo**   **sting**   **imitation**

[2 marks]

D.4 What is the tonality of the excerpt?

[1 mark]

Total: 5 marks

AREA OF STUDY 4:
Music for theatre

Question A

Track 70

The excerpt is from Kurt Weill's *Street scene*. The song is called 'What good would the moon be?' The lyrics for the excerpt are below.

1 What good would the moon be
2 Unless the right one shared its beams?
3 What good would dreams come true be
4 If love wasn't in those dreams?

5 And a primrose path
6 What would be the fun
7 Of walking down a path like that
8 Without the right one?

A.1 Describe fully the melody on 'What good would the moon' at the beginning of the excerpt.

_____

_____ [2 marks]

A.2 Which added note is heard in the chord under 'moon be' (in line 1, underlined above)? Underline your answer.

    6th   **minor 7th**   **major 7th**   **9th** [1 mark]

A.3 What is the melodic interval between the notes on 'the' and 'fun' at the end of line 6 (underlined)?

_____ [1 mark]

A.4 Describe the rhythm on 'down a path' (in line 7, underlined above).

_____ [1 mark]

Total: 5 marks

OPTIONAL AREAS OF STUDY (AOS): ADDITIONAL QUESTIONS

Question B

Track 71

The excerpt is from Schönberg and Boublil's musical *Les Misérables*. The song is called 'Drink with me'. The lyrics for the excerpt are below.

1. Drink with me to days gone by
2. Sing with me the songs we knew
3. Here's to pretty girls who went to our heads
4. Here's to witty girls who went to our beds
5. Here's to them
6. And here's to you

B.1 What cadence can be heard at the end of line 1?

[1 mark]

B.2 Give the locations (by writing the words on which they occur) of **TWO** different dominant 7th chords heard in the excerpt.

[2 marks]

B.3 Describe how the melodies of lines 3 and 4 (underlined above) relate to one another.

[1 mark]

B.4 Which instrument plays flowing quavers in the accompaniment?

[1 mark]

Total: 5 marks

Question C

Track 72

The excerpt is from Rodgers and Hammerstein's musical *The sound of music*. The song is called 'My favourite things'. The lyrics for the excerpt are below.

1. Raindrops on roses and whiskers on kittens
2. Bright copper kettles and warm woollen mittens
3. Brown paper packages tied up with strings
4. These are a few of my favourite things

5. Cream coloured ponies and crisp apple strudels
6. Doorbells and sleigh bells and schnitzel with noodles
7. Wild geese that fly with the moon on their wings

C.1 What is the interval heard on the words 'warm' and 'woollen' (in line 2, underlined above)?

[1 mark]

AS/A LEVEL MUSIC LISTENING TESTS

C.2 The lyrics of the third phrase are 'Brown paper packages tied up with strings' (underlined above). What chord progression can be heard accompanying this phrase?

[1 mark]

C.3 What cadence can be heard on 'favourite things' at the end of the first verse (underlined above)?

[1 mark]

C.4 How does the texture change at the second verse?

[1 mark]

C.5 Which instrument doubles the melody on 'Wild geese that fly with the moon on their wings' (in line 7, underlined above)?

[1 mark]

Total: 5 marks

Question D

Track 73

The excerpt is from Jason Robert Brown's musical *The last five years*. The song is called 'I can do better than that'.

D.1 Which **TWO** instruments play the bass line in the excerpt?

[2 marks]

D.2 What is the interval between the first two notes sung in the excerpt?

[1 mark]

D.3 Which **TWO** of the following describe the chords played by the guitar and right hand of the piano in the excerpt? Underline your answers.

played on beats 1 and 3   **played on beats 2 and 4**

same pitch throughout   **change pitch every 2 bars**

change pitch every 4 bars

[2 marks]

Total: 5 marks

AREA OF STUDY 5:
Jazz

Question A

Track 74

The excerpt is from Gwilym Simcock's 'Above the sun'.

A.1 Which **TWO** of the following instruments can be heard in the excerpt? Underline your answers.

soprano saxophone   alto saxophone

tenor saxophone   clarinet   bass clarinet   [2 marks]

A.2 What is the harmonic interval between the melody and the bass at 0:37?

_____
                                                                   [1 mark]

A.3 Complete the rhythm heard in the piano chords between the two solos (at 0:54).

                                                                   [1 mark]

A.4 Which of the following chords is heard at the very end of the excerpt? Underline your answer.

dominant 7th   minor 9th   major 7th   minor   [1 mark]

Total: 5 marks

AS/A LEVEL MUSIC LISTENING TESTS

Question B

Track 75

The excerpt is from Miles Davis's 'Walkin''.

B.1 Which of the following structural elements is **NOT** heard in the excerpt?

    break   **head**   **solo**   **fours** [1 mark]

B.2 Name the technique used by the trumpet at 0:21.

_____ [1 mark]

B.3 Complete the following grid to show the harmonic progression in the four bars from 0.14.

bar 1	bar 2	bar 3	bar 4
I			I

[2 marks]

B.4 Which part of the drum kit can be heard on every beat of the trumpet solo?

_____ [1 mark]

Total: 5 marks

Question C

Track 76

The excerpt is from Pat Metheny's 'Chris'.

C.1 What chord is created when the bass reaches its third pitch?

_____ [1 mark]

C.2 The melody enters at 0:17. On which degree of the scale does it enter?

_____ [1 mark]

C.3 Circle the **TWO** pitches of the opening bass line which remain unchanged as the bass line repeats throughout the excerpt.

[2 marks]

C.4 In which decade was the excerpt composed? Underline your answer.

    1940s   **1960s**   **1980s**   **2000s** [1 mark]

Total: 5 marks

Question D

Track 77

The excerpt is from Louis Armstrong's 'Struttin' with some barbecue'.

D.1 Which **TWO** of the following describe the opening melody? Underline your answers.

    ascending major scale   **uses blue notes**   **syncopated**

    ends on the dominant   **played on the clarinet**   [2 marks]

D.2 Name the melodic embellishment heard in the trombone part at 0:14, 0:16 and 0:19 (and later in the excerpt also).

_____ [1 mark]

D.3 How many bars are there in the excerpt?

_____ [1 mark]

D.4 Describe the bass line in the final bar of the excerpt.

_____ [1 mark]

Total: 5 marks

AREA OF STUDY 6: Contemporary traditional music

Question A

Track 78

The excerpt is from Anoushka Shankar's 'Boat to Nowhere' from the album *Land of gold*.

A.1 Below is the outline of the opening melody (heard in repeated notes from 1:20–1:45). Add **TWO** suitable accidentals to complete the outline.

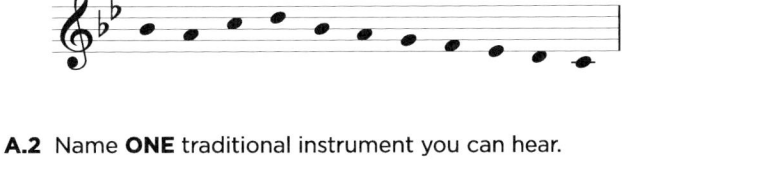

[2 marks]

A.2 Name **ONE** traditional instrument you can hear.

[1 mark]

A.3 Name **ONE** non-traditional instrument you can hear.

[1 mark]

A.4 Which of the following is **NOT** a feature of this excerpt? Underline your answer.

drone   **tala**   **alap**   **raga**

[1 mark]

Total: 5 marks

OPTIONAL AREAS OF STUDY (AOS): ADDITIONAL QUESTIONS

Question B

Track 79

The excerpt is from the song 'Medo', sung by Mariza.

B.1 What style of song is this?

_____
[1 mark]

B.2 Add **TWO** missing chord names for the four bars from 0:13, using Roman numeral analysis.

bar 1   iv_____

bar 2   i

bar 3   i

bar 4   _____

[2 marks]

B.3 What chord is heard on the last beat of the bar **AFTER** the table above (at 0:28)?

_____
[1 mark]

B.4 Which of the following is the correct bass tag at the end of this excerpt? Tick your answer.

A

B

C

D

[1 mark]

Total: 5 marks

Question C

Track 80

The excerpt is from 'Primavera Porteña' by Astor Piazzolla.

C.1 Name **TWO** special tango techniques used by the violin in this excerpt.

_____

_____ [2 marks]

C.2 Name **ONE** special tango technique used by the piano/bass in this excerpt.

_____ [1 mark]

C.3 Give a suitable time signature for the excerpt.

_____ [1 mark]

C.4 Underline the correct chord progression on which the excerpt is based.

    i – VII – VI – V   i – VII – ivb – V   i – vb – VI – V   i – vb – ivb – V   [1 mark]

Total: 5 marks

Question D

Track 81

The excerpt is from 'Kora Bali' played by Toumani Diabaté and Ballake Sissoko.

D.1 Name **ONE** special playing technique you can hear from either kora player.

_____ [1 mark]

D.2 Which **ONE** of the following descriptions is **NOT** true of the melody? Underline your answer.

    modal   **heard in octaves**   **embellished**   **conjunct**   [1 mark]

D.3 What happens to the tempo and pulse at 0:41?

_____

_____ [2 marks]

D.4 How is this signalled?

_____ [1 mark]

Total: 5 marks

OPTIONAL AREAS OF STUDY (AOS): ADDITIONAL QUESTIONS

A LEVEL ONLY

AREA OF STUDY 7:
Art music since 1910

Question A

Track 82

The excerpt is from Shostakovich's String quartet no. 8, first movement.

A.1 The opening four notes of the excerpt are written below. Circle the incorrect note.

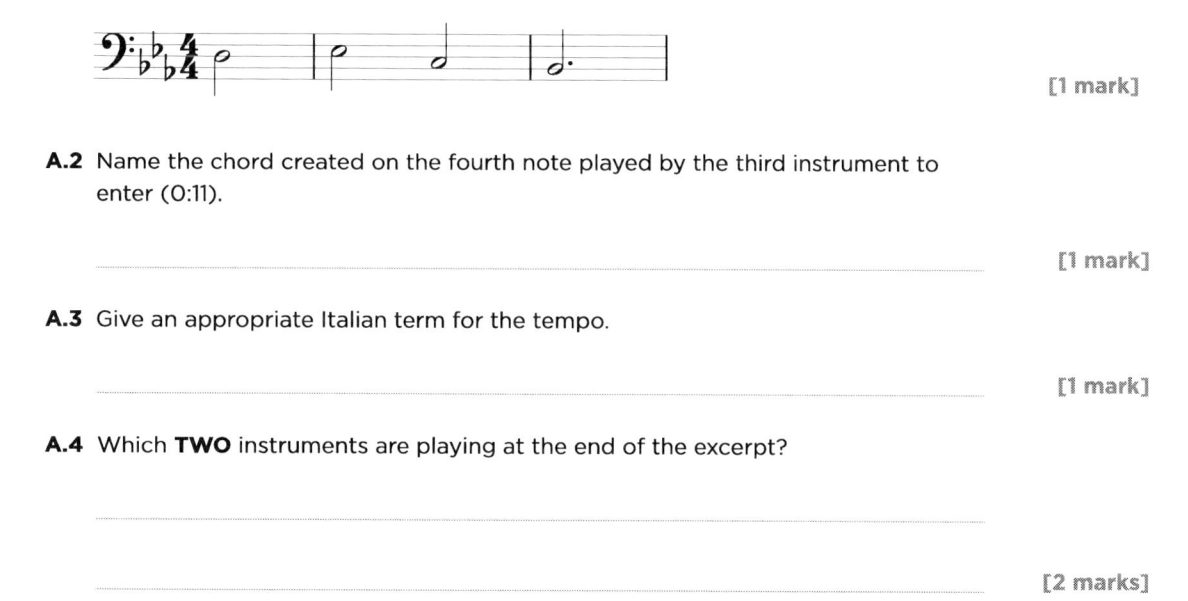

[1 mark]

A.2 Name the chord created on the fourth note played by the third instrument to enter (0:11).

_____

[1 mark]

A.3 Give an appropriate Italian term for the tempo.

_____

[1 mark]

A.4 Which **TWO** instruments are playing at the end of the excerpt?

_____

_____

[2 marks]

Total: 5 marks

Question B

Track 83

The excerpt is from Steve Reich's 'Clapping music'.

B.1 Complete the **THREE** quaver beats in the following, which is heard at the beginning of the excerpt.

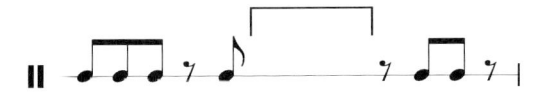

[3 marks]

B.2 How many times is the music above heard before there is any change in the music?

[1 mark]

B.3 Describe **ONE** way in which the music changes at the end of the excerpt.

[1 mark]

Total: 5 marks

Question C

Track 84

The excerpt is from James Macmillan's Oboe concerto, first movement.

C.1 Name fully the melodic interval heard between the first two pitches (third and fourth notes) of the excerpt.

[1 mark]

C.2 Name the instrument that enters with the melody at 0:01.

[1 mark]

C.3 What type of chord would be created if the first four notes of the oboe line were played simultaneously?

[1 mark]

C.4 Which instrument doubles the very high note played by the oboe near the end of the excerpt?

[1 mark]

C.5 Which technique does the doubling instrument use at the end of the excerpt?

[1 mark]

Total: 5 marks

OPTIONAL AREAS OF STUDY (AOS): ADDITIONAL QUESTIONS

Question D

Track 85

The excerpt is from Messiaen's 'Le merle noir'.

D.1 Describe the opening piano statement.

_____

_____ [2 marks]

D.2 Describe the articulation heard in the melodic fragment at 0:17.

_____ [1 mark]

D.3 Name the instrumental technique heard on the flute at 0:34.

_____ [1 mark]

D.4 Which of the following melody lines is played by the piano when it first enters after the monophonic flute line?

A ☐

B ☐

C ☐

D ☐

[1 mark]

Total: 5 marks

Answers

Introduction

Mark schemes are difficult documents to compile and we often find ourselves at odds with their content, particularly on open-ended questions.

It is important to note that mark schemes are working documents and during the examining process they do change and expand – examiners are not mind-readers and sometimes a perfectly acceptable answer will not have originally been included. In these mark schemes, particularly those for the longer questions, we do not claim to have listed every possible answer.

Be assured that as examiners mark they DO have musical scores open in front of them and will verify responses not originally in the mark scheme. This is not to say that all *true* facts about an excerpt will necessarily gain a mark – some true facts may not gain marks, either because they do not answer the question or because they do not show a sophisticated enough response.

Further guidance on mark schemes in general can be found in the Sample Assessment Material in the AQA AS and A Level Specifications.

Mark band descriptors for long answer questions

Marks out of 10

9 – 10 marks	A comprehensive and authoritative response that is consistently coherent and logically structured
7 – 8 marks	A wide-ranging and confident response that is mostly coherent and well structured
5 – 6 marks	A relevant response despite some inaccuracy/omission and weaknesses in terms of coherency and structure
3 – 4 marks	A limited response with some inaccuracy/omission and a lack of clarity
1 – 2 marks	A rudimentary response
0 marks	No work submitted or worthy of credit

Marks out of 5

5 marks	An authoritative response that is consistently coherent and logically structured
3 – 4 marks	A wide-ranging response that is mostly coherent and well structured
1 – 2 marks	A limited response with some significant inaccuracy/omission and a lack of clarity
0 marks	No work submitted or worthy of credit

AS Level full paper

AS Section A

1.1 minor

1.2 (perfect) 4th

1.3 turn

1.4 it goes into triplets (semiquavers)

2.1 diminished

2.2 bass

2.3 [music notation: 4/4 dotted quarter, eighth, dotted quarter, eighth] [2 marks]

3 [music notation with text "Ist mir denn kein Herz ge-ge-ben?" and "Ich bin auch den Maed-chen gut,"]
[1 mark for each of 6 pitches correct]

4a texture
- starts monophonic (with fugue subject)
- single violin line to start
- oboe joins (with fugue answer)
- contrapuntal texture created
- other parts continue the fugal texture

instrumentation
- oboe
- strings
- continuo played by cello and harpsichord

melody
- conjunct movement to start
- leaps of 4th and octave
- sequential patterns
- tonal answer
- trill in oboe

tonality
- starts in tonic
- reaches dominant by the end of the first oboe phrase
- returns to the tonic

rhythm
- tied notes
- flourishes

harmony
- tonic and dominant
- suspensions
- Any other valid points [maximum 10 marks]

4b texture
- sparse homophony
- solo singer with strings and harpsichord
- string interjections

structure
- recitative (secco and accompliano)
- melody
- appoggiatura
- lots of conjunct movement
- some leaps
- repeated notes

harmony
- diminished chord is first heard
- strong cadences
- dissonance resolved by step
- Any other valid points [maximum 10 marks]

5.1 **C** is correct

5.2 4/4

5.3 5th

5.4 (perfect) 4th higher

5.5 major

6.1 (internal) pedal

6.2 3rds

6.3 **A** is correct

6.4 drums [1], electric guitar [1], (synth) strings [1], synthesiser/organ [1] [maximum 2 marks]

7.1 plagal (E♭ minor – B♭ minor chords)

7.2 major (A♭ major)

7.3 (perfect) 5th

7.4 vocals fed into a vocoder [1]; repeated chord sequence [1]

8 gospel elements might include:
- use of a piano riff
- thickly harmonised backing vocals or layered/multi-tracked vocals in parallel chords
- use of call and response between lead vocals and backing vocals
- use of hand claps
- (synth) string pad chords supporting the vocals
- low organ-like bass line in chorus

soul elements might include:
- melismatic vocal lines
- wide vocal range

down-tempo feel
impassioned vocal delivery

pop/R'n'B elements might include:
dance-style synth riff on the chorus
drum fills to support the hand claps
verse-chorus structure (though this could easily be applied to 'soul' as well)
Any other valid points [maximum 10 marks]

9.1 major (with added 9th)

9.2 **D** is correct

9.3 tremolo or tremolando

9.4 pedal/drone; the note A is heard throughout the excerpt

9.5 minor

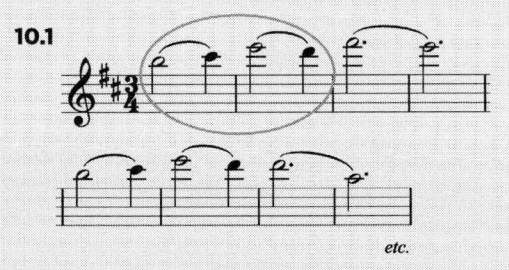

10.1

bars 1 and 2 are repeated in bars 5 and 6

10.2 (solo) violin [1], flute [1] [maximum 1 mark]

10.3 harp

10.4 waltz

11.1 3rd

11.2 major

11.3 tambourine; accept cymbal

11.4 delay effect, cross rhythm

12 The overall feeling of tension and frenetic energy are suggested by the following:

ominous opening four-note motif in low brass; motif spans a tritone (an interval that is unsettling) and includes a piano tremolo on final note
use of string tremolo
string effects in extreme high register (glissando, tremolo, trills)
rapidly changing textures
fast, compound-time bass figure; transferred later to upper strings in a different key
percussive stings punctuating phrases
rapid chromatic scales up and down in lower strings with timpani/bass drum roll as background texture: creates an unsettled or tense mood
opening four-note motif repeating in high string octaves with *glissando* for extra creepy effect

urgent-sounding trumpet melody suggests distress through angular contours and spiky rhythm
four-note motif heard in strings as sustained notes to build up a dissonant chord
low, slow-moving brass chords
oscillating semitone motif in strings and flutes
Any other valid points [maximum 10 marks]

13.1 first inversion major chord

13.2 descending scale

13.3 augmented 4th/diminished 5th/tritone

13.4 rising 5th at start [1], first two notes are the same each time [1] [maximum 1 mark]

13.5 semitone/minor 2nd

14.1 harp, clarinet

14.2 'me'

14.3 **C** is correct

14.4 'in'

15.1 imperfect

15.2 octave

15.3
[2 marks]

15.4 pizzicato

16 **texture**
second singer taking over (interrupting)
counterpoint of voices
simple accompaniment allows voices to be heard clearly
instrumentation/timbre
'gentle' vocal sound at start
replaced by an 'edge' to the vocal sound
deep bass line
high-register shimmerings

rhythm
persistent pulsing
bass playing on beats 4 and 1
quaver+two semiquaver rhythm on first beat has martial/military sound

melody
two distinct melody lines
higher register as tension rises
repeated notes give insistence

dynamics
begins piano/softly
crescendo into the contrapuntal section
Any other valid points [maximum 10 marks]

AS/A LEVEL MUSIC LISTENING TESTS

17.1 D is correct

17.2 second time the final note is repeated

17.3 4½ beats

17.4 major 7th chord

17.5 Intro AABA

18.1 (perfect) 4th

18.2 trumpet, alto saxophone

18.3 14

18.4 crescendo

19.1

[1 mark for each of 2 correct accidentals inserted]

19.2 7 (drum kit, alto saxophone, trumpet, double bass, piano, tenor saxophone, electric guitar)

19.3 accept 210–240

19.4 major

20 **instrumentation/timbre**
use of Latin American percussion instruments
bongos, congos, shakers
jazz drum kit
rhythm
emphasis on beats 2 and 4
semiquavers in percussion
two semiquavers+quaver rhythm, typical of Latin American music
syncopation in the melody
melody
repeated melody lines
emphasis on tonic and flattened leading note
harmony
extended chords used
harmonic oscillation (between V^{11} and Im^7)
texture
strong bass line
chords in piano
melody on guitar
typical rhythm section
Any other valid points [maximum 10 marks]

21.1 5th/dominant

21.2 (minor) 6th

21.3 falsetto

21.4 mediant

21.5 octaves

22.1 E and D above the given G

22.2 IV

22.3 G minor

22.4 drone

23.1 piano [1], double bass (acoustic/upright) [1]

23.2 moderato, medium tempo, allegro, fast or other suitable term; no extreme tempos

23.3 (perfect) 5th (D to A inclusive)

23.4 nine

24 West African elements that can be heard on the recording include:
kora
djembes/hand drums
balafon (pitched percussion instrument heard at the start)
ngoni (six-string plucked guitar-like instrument)
vocals (main vocal and backing vocals – and the interaction between the two, though not quite 'call and response')
use of repeated rhythmic patterns/ostinatos
strong rhythmic drive of the track owes as much to African traditions as to the other world styles espoused
Other aspects of the recording include:
use of brass (trumpets and trombones) for rhythmic stabs (as in funk/soul/jazz/salsa traditions)
electric guitar used to amplify and complement kora figures
drum kit used in addition to hand drums
electric bass grooves added with the entry of drum kit
repeating short chord progression and layers of rhythmic ostinato are also common features of many Latin American styles and this is clearly an influence on this track
Any other valid points [maximum 10 marks]

AS Section B

25.1 it is the ritornello theme

25.2 E minor

25.3 major [1] 3rd [1]

25.4 one

25.5 perfect

25.6 canon [at the unison]

25.7 **harmony**
relative minor at start of excerpt (B minor; tonic is D major)
tonic and dominant (of relative minor) at start

run of perfect cadences bars 53–56
static harmony bars 57–59
perfect cadence at bars 61–62 into relative minor
dominant pedal at end of excerpt

texture
in octaves at opening
same as opening of movement (without solo rising arpeggio)
solo line with rest of orchestra at opening
drops to solo and violins
canon towards the end

melody
lots of upper auxiliary notes
jumps of octaves (typical Vivaldi style)
rising chromatic scale
use of episode
trills
Any other valid points [maximum 10 marks]

26.1 major

26.2 bar 9 or bar 12

26.3 ii⁷b or F minor 7 1st inversion [2 marks]

26.4 interrupted

26.5 bar 16

26.6 homophonic or melody and accompaniment

26.7 rhythm
every quaver has movement
fast tempo
anacrusis gives an impetus
change to four quavers at beginning of bar heightens excitement
quaver rests in violins give impetus
motor rhythm in melody

metre
2/2 has an inherent drive

harmony
harmonic rhythm increases (from a change each bar to a change each half-bar)
strong cadences, imperfect and perfect (interrupted as mentioned above)
chromaticism at the end of the excerpt gives momentum and energy

melody
repeated notes give a sense of energetically spoken words
reaches a high G at bar 10, which raises the emotive effect
chromatic lines at the end
much use of appoggiatura
Any other valid points [maximum 10 marks]

AS additional dictation questions

A

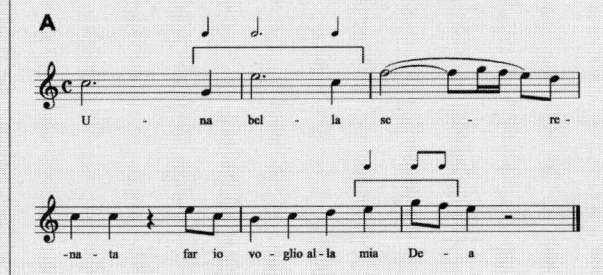

[1 mark for each of 6 pitches correct]

B

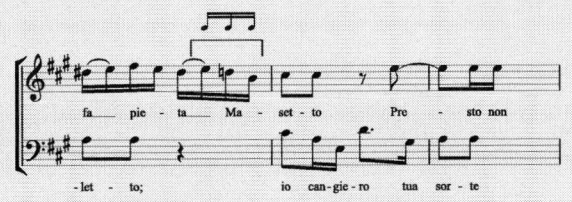

[1 mark for each of 6 pitches correct]

C

[1 mark for each of 6 pitches correct]

AS additional Section B questions

25.1 bar 2, beat 2

25.2 upper auxiliary note

25.3 A major

25.4 antiphony

25.5 4–3 [1] suspension [1]

25.6 anticipatory note

25.7 Mention should be made of the capabilities of the natural trumpet and the harmonic series.

melody
use of arpeggiated figures
perfect 5ths
high register allowing more harmonics

rhythm
fanfare type rhythms
motor rhythm
rests included – important for brass players

texture
at times fragmented

antiphonal texture allows breaks for the player
homophonic to start
imitative
almost canonic
Any other valid points [maximum 10 marks]

26.1 188, 196

26.2 1st inversion major chord, F/A, tonic b

26.3 the first is rising, the second falling [1]; the first is augmented 4th, the second perfect 4th [1]

26.4 recitative bar 7

26.5 recitative bar 11 final quaver; aria bars 22, 112

26.6 F major

26.7 **tempo**
becomes set (not free as in preceding recitative) as Figaro realises the situation
changes reflect the text at the end of the recitative
flowing in the cavatina

harmony
wide range of harmony in the recitative reflects the unfolding narrative
cavatina is diatonic, reflecting a firmness of mind

melody
rising melodies in the recitative reflect questions (e.g. 'Basilio?')
simple rhythms and largely conjunct melody in opening of cavatina
sequential use of melody in first two phrases

metre
dance-like, lilting minuet in the aria
triple time
these highlight the metaphor in the libretto
Any other valid points [maximum 10 marks]

A Level full paper

A Level Section A

1.1 perfect 5th

1.2 octave higher [1], quieter dynamic [1]

1.3 flattened leading note major

2

[1 mark for each of 6 pitches correct]

3 **texture**
violins
instrumental interjections
melody and accompaniment

structure
instrumental introduction playing the opening vocal melody
return to the opening melody

melody
repetition of phrases
use of arpeggiation
syncopation incorporated
scalic rises to the cadence in main theme

harmony
strong cadences
tonic–dominant prominent
modulation to related key
Any other valid points [maximum 10 marks]

4.1 octave

4.2 plagal

4.3 five (F#, A, E, B, D)

4.4 glissando

5.1 **A** is correct

5.2 filter (this is opened up towards the kick entry)

5.3 hi-hat [1], rim shot [2]
(For information: the synth rhythm negates the need for hi-hat, and the kick is partnered with what sounds like an 8-bit hand clap rather than snare; there are also real hand claps towards the end of the excerpt.)

AS/A LEVEL MUSIC LISTENING TESTS

6 **reggae elements in the song might include:**
   heavy swing/compound time feel
   emphasis on offbeat (swung quavers)
   short, rhythmic chops in guitar/bass accompaniment
   other percussion used in addition to drums
   use of backing singers singing in block harmonies
   horn stabs and riffs used to punctuate vocal lines (this may also be said to be an element of Stevie Wonder's own style)
   organ chords played on third beat of bar
   simple chord progressions and mainly triadic harmony
   reverb and compression on vocals

   elements of Stevie Wonder's own style might include:
   distinctive high vocal lines, including improvisation around main melody
   strong emphasis on keyboard lines (Stevie Wonder's own instrument) to thicken the bass riff: clavinet, (Rhodes) electric piano, organ
   extended riff in octaves for the band (15 seconds in): demonstration of tight musicianship and technical skill
   some use of extended triad harmonies (e.g. dominant 9th – F^9)
   horn stabs and riffs used to punctuate vocal lines (this may also be said to be an element of reggae style)
   Any other valid points [maximum 10 marks]

7.1 $\frac{3}{4}$

7.2 (tonic) pedal

7.3 interrupted

7.4 first inversion

8.1 D is correct

8.2 sequence

8.3 pizzicato [1], tremolo [1], sul ponticello [1] [maximum 2 marks]

9 The main thing here is the ominous nature of Gort's first appearance and the power of the visor ray. Points might include:

   synchronisation
   loud opening serves as a sting to the cut to Gort (information given in rubric)
   timings given for the ray-blasts are accompanied by sting chords in brass (*sfp* with crescendo), also articulated with suspended cymbal hit and roll
   final ray-blast accompanied by additional rhythmic stabs (more powerful blast to eradicate the tank) with piano and cymbal hits adding extra attack

   melody
   low tessitura for melody: trombones, tubas, low strings, piano
   low theremin (accept electronic instrument or synthesiser) also used to punctuate changes in pitch, with glissando between notes for creepy effect; also wide vibrato of theremin is a creepy and ominous sound
   melody is in long note values/slow tempo, creating a ponderous and menacing mood
   melody starts low but gets progressively higher before subsiding again to lower pitch; implies increased tension/ominous mood
   frequent use of tritone interval in melody
   melody suggests atonality (though C can be heard as a sort of pitch centre) and is almost dodecaphonic

   texture
   opening melody is heard in octaves with no other accompaniment
   sting chords used later for appearance of ray gun
   percussion (bass drum) punctuates off-beats or midway points between melody notes
   bass melody continues during the sting chords in slow-moving notes, implies relentless and invincible robot

   rhythm
   slow, ponderous tempo suggests the sheer size of the robot and slow, menacing footsteps
   more intricate rhythmic fragments in piano accompany quieter passages before the ray blast is unleashed; suggestion of tension and menace, anticipation
   repeated stab chords at shorter note values/faster tempo suggest power and threatening behaviour

   harmony
   stark octave texture at beginning has no obvious harmonic parallel
   minor triad with major seventh used for ray blasts (pungent and dissonant against underlying bass line, suggesting the searing heat of the ray)

   Any other valid points [maximum 10 marks]

10.1 dominant/5th

10.2 C is correct

10.3 perfect 4th

10.4 1st inversion minor

11.1 false relation

11.2 augmented

11.3

[1 mark for getting first 5 notes correct, 1 mark for getting final note correct]

12 Reference should be made to the fact that this meeting has created a sense of turmoil for Chris, as shown in the lyrics: 'Nothing here makes sense' and 'Why, God, why?'

melody
gradual ascension of tessitura showing rising emotions

timbre
use of spoken word on 'ringing'

harmony
4–3 dissonance used (including tritone)
9th on 'Why'
imperfect cadence at end of refrain reflecting the feeling that things are being left open-ended

rhythm
towards the end of the excerpt the bass and rhythm section increase the number of notes per bar

dynamics
higher dynamics as the song continues, particularly on 'Why, God'

texture
sparse texture at start
depth added at refrain to reflect depth of feelings
Any other valid points [maximum 10 marks]

13.1 monophonic

13.2 **C** is correct

13.3 sequence

13.4 dominant

14.1 final note (G)

14.2 minor 9th

14.3 lower pitch [1], embellished melody [1], use of ornaments [1] [maximum 2 marks]

15 harmony
reharmonisation
modal harmony
quartal harmony
rising parallel chords in accompaniment

melody
embellishment of original
use of imitation/countermelody from other members of the ensemble
ghosted notes
improvisation around the melody
use of modes

rhythm
walking bass
swung quavers
faster tempo

texture
jazz instrumentation (not orchestral as original)
Any other valid points [maximum 10 marks]

16.1 kora [1], guitar [1] [maximum 1 mark]

16.2 6/8 or 12/8

16.3 subdominant/4th/IV

16.4 modulation

17.1 minor

17.2 major

17.3 any two from: piano, double bass, electric guitar, violin [maximum 2 marks]

18 Bellowhead is a group well known for its energetic interpretations of traditional folk songs; here, elements from 1970s funk and disco seem woven into the mix.

traditional elements might include:
slow-moving oboe melody in introduction, accompanied by accordion, taken up by a pair of fiddles before first vocal entry
retention of original melody, which is largely untouched
use of sustained fiddle chords in the refrain
use of choral repeat (in octaves) of refrain in the third time (call and response)
modal harmony/melody
repeated chords before vocal entry are bare 5ths only
sousaphone (accept tuba) used as a main bass instrument

more modern elements might include:
up-tempo feel, use of repeated notes and quick brass licks in introduction
repeated notes on downbeat to punctuate introduction
disco-style repeated hi-hat semiquavers with emphasis on each beat
after first and second refrain, a stylistic change with rapid, funk-style octave riffs in

brass, heavily distorted electric guitar chops, and brass and string stabs in the manner of disco/funk

syncopated brass chords in third verse add weight and momentum

Any other valid points [maximum 10 marks]

19.1 11

19.2 A is correct

19.3 a chord is added

19.4 maraca (accept 'shaker')

20.1 xylophone [1], clarinet [1]

20.2 major

20.3 I – V – I – V

21 Reference should be made to the fact that this piece does not have the feeling of celebration associated with the original theme.

harmony
opening chords played low in the register
repeated chord pattern ending on minor chord
melody reharmonised
use of open 5th
dissonance prominent
use of pedal blurs harmony and adds dissonance

melody
melody not heard at beginning
melody fragmented
exact copy of original

tonality
minor inflections
ambiguity

dynamics
quiet dynamics to open
dynamics rises towards the end of the excerpt
Any other valid points [maximum 10 marks]

A Level Section B

22.1 1st inversion chord

22.2 perfect octave

22.3 much unharmonised single line (doubled) music
1st violin and flute in 3rds
antiphonal effect
inner string lines drop out at the solo episode (bar 16)
independent line in the accompaniment
two-part texture throughout
Any other valid points [maximum 5 marks]

22.4 Mention should be made that the movement is a ritornello, and the excerpt should be discussed in that context.

melody
repeated motifs
unison/octave playing in orchestra
melody heard in thirds in solo violin/violin 1
ornamentation used
descending concertino versus rising solo
oscillating semiquavers (written out trills)
use of sequence
rising 4th

rhythm
rhythmic ideas repeated
two semiquaver and quaver figure used many times
dotted figures used
repeated quavers

structure
ritornello (first bar always the same figuration with changes in subsequent bars)
episode
Any other valid points [maximum 10 marks]

23.1 supertonic and dominant/2nd and 5th

23.2 VIIb in A major/first inversion diminished

23.3 **melody and accompaniment**
use of countermelody
doubling of melody (in first violin)
wind expands the texture at particular points (often cadences)
2nd violin outlining harmony with arpeggiated figure
bassoon and cellos working together
horns play pedal
Any other valid points [maximum 5 marks]

23.4 Mention should be made of the dramatic setting: measuring up for their marital home and the roles they both play.

melody
two melodies, one for each singer
jumps for Figaro
conjunct movement for Susanna
Figaro goes on to sing Susanna's flowing melody
depiction of drama in melodic moments

AS/A LEVEL MUSIC LISTENING TESTS

texture
interaction between the melodic parts
use of pedal (bass and internal)
use of wind as Susanna enters

rhythm
measured crotchets for Figaro
flowing quaver movement for Susanna
triplets motion
orchestral movement adds to the momentum of the music
Any other valid points [maximum 10 marks]

24.1 3rd inversion dominant 7th or E⁷/D or V⁷d

24.2 [compound] augmented 4th

24.3 repeated rhythms (with different melodic lines)
cross-rhythm used
quaver movement throughout
crotchet movement in second melodic idea
tying across bars
use of anacrusis
Any other valid points [maximum 5 marks]

24.4 To gain top marks, mention should be made of the typical features of Chopin and Grieg and which of these are *not* heard in this excerpt (e.g. drone; ornamentation).

harmony
root position tonic at start
tonic pedal used in opening
secondary dominants used
chromaticism (examples needed)

melody
repeated opening melodic fragment with an augmented intervallic leap
falling by step, then rising by leap as opening idea
appoggiaturic second idea (aided by hairpin dynamics)

texture
melody and accompaniment
flowing quaver movement in accompaniment
compass of 4 octaves
inner chords
Any other valid points
[maximum 10 marks]

A Level additional dictation questions

A

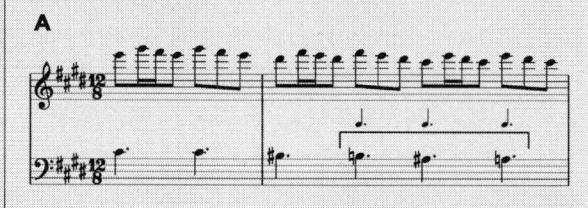

[1 mark for each of 6 pitches correct]

B

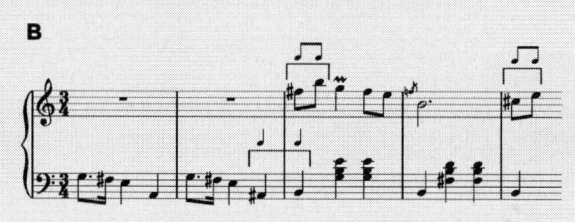

[1 mark for each of 6 pitches correct]

C

[1 mark for each of 6 pitches correct]

A Level additional Section B questions

22.1 G major

22.2 descending sequence

22.3 Answers might mention the typical resolution of dissonance by step and the use of both accented and unaccented dissonance.

Many examples of the following can be found and should be included: passing note; auxiliary note; suspension; and appoggiatura.

Any other valid points [maximum 5 marks]

22.4 For top marks, reference must be must to the writing of other composers (probably Vivaldi and Purcell) giving some specific similarities (e.g. use of continuo in texture, sequence in melody) and differences (e.g. flow versus repetition in melody and rhythm)

texture
first violin and solo violin double
violins interject on longer solo notes
continuo plays throughout
inner parts with some flow
sparse at bar 25 as solo violin plays alone
counterpoint between solo and continuo

melody
flowing
use of repeated notes
use of sequence
some large leaps
some awkward intervals in the solo line

rhythm
quaver-based melody
ties across beats
jaunty crotchet and quaver rhythm within compound time
anacrusis
Any other valid points [maximum 10 marks]

23.1 tonic pedal

23.2 D major/tonic

23.3 predominance of strings
wind with some melodic lines
wind doubling of strings for colour
timpani used for accenting, particularly towards cadence points
brass used for filling harmony
flute countermelody
largely homophonic texture
Any other valid points [maximum 5 marks]

23.4 Mention should be made that the opera is a comedy and the pace and verve (or similar) of the overture set the scene for the fast-paced, action-packed drama.

melody
semitones in this major tonality give a sense of comedic flexibility (particularly in bar 4)
rhythmic and melodic 'bursts' hint at dramaticism
phrase lengths throw the music slightly off kilter, reflecting comedy

harmony
major tonality
use of suspension
pedal notes

chromaticism in harmony as well (e.g. augmented 6th chords, descending semitones)

texture
opening theme doubled by bassoons (the most comic of instruments?)
opening played in unison/octaves
contrast with the second section of first theme
Any other valid points [maximum 10 marks]

24.1 major chord on the flattened submediant

24.2 [Compound] diminished 5th

24.3 Mention should be made of pedals/drones/open 5ths as part of the folky/nationalistic tendencies of Grieg.
tonic pedal at start
dominant pedal at bar 6
open 5ths (many examples)
harmonic colour added by non-diatonic chords
use of circle of 5ths
suspensions
Any other valid points [maximum 5 marks]

24.4 Mention should be made of nationalistic and dance elements in this and the rest of the movement; answers should also mention the overall structure and how this excerpt fits within that context.

melody
dance-like quality to some of the melodic lines
use of sequence (extensive)
ornamentation
large range

rhythm
use of syncopation
use of ties
strong march feel
melody starting after a quaver rest
structure
ABAB coda

dynamics
fortepiano
diminuendo
ppp sections
crescendo molto
fortissimo at the end of the excerpt into the next section
Any other valid points [maximum 10 marks]

Optional Areas of Study (AoS): additional questions

AoS 2: Pop music

A.1 three (D♯, C♯, B)

A.2 3rd/mediant

A.3 mediant/iii/D♯m/D♯ minor

A.4 chromaticism, plagal cadence

B.1 F, C/E (accept F major and C major 1st inversion, but chord symbols should really be used)

B.2 (perfect) 4th

B.3 Gm/G minor; accept subdominant

B.4 synth (lead sound)
drum machine/drum samples/synth drums. Do not accept 'drum kit' or 'drums': at this level, candidates should spot that these are not *real* drums

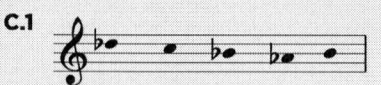

C.1

[1 mark for each of 2 correct accidentals added]

C.2 line 3/third line; last note here is C not B♭

C.3 major 7th

C.4 rising/ascending scale

D.1 delay

D.2 (perfect) 5th

D.3 portamento, filtering

D.4 minor

AoS 3: Music for media

A.1 three

A.2 any two from: horns, trombone, tuba, snare/side drum, timpani, bass drum

A.3 4/4

A.4 3/4

B.1 (major) 6th

B.2 C is correct

B.3 sequence, canon

B.4 electric guitar

C.1 triplets or syncopation

C.2 con sordino/with mutes

C.3 oboe, clarinet

C.4 inversion

D.1 flute

D.2 (compound) minor 7th

D.3 drone, tremolo

D.4 modal (For reference, the mode is Aeolian; ♮VII used consistently.)

AoS 4: Music for theatre

A.1 ascending [1] chromatic scale [1]

A.2 6th

A.3 minor 3rd

A.4 dotted

B.1 perfect

B.2 days, songs, pretty girls, witty girls, here's (in the last line). [maximum 2 marks]

B.3 sequential

B.4 guitar (classical)

C.1 [perfect] 4th

C.2 circle of 5ths

C.3 imperfect

C.4 continuous inner parts [1] or more rhythmic activity (oom-cha-cha) [1] [maximum 1 mark]

C.5 flute

D.1 piano, double bass

D.2 minor 3rd

D.3 played on beats 2 and 4; same pitch throughout

AoS 5: Jazz

A.1 bass clarinet and soprano saxophone

A.2 octave

A.3

A.4 minor 9th

B.1 fours

B.2 ghosting

B.3 bar 2: IV; bar 3: I

B.4 ride cymbal

C.1 major 7th

C.2 dominant/5th

AS/A LEVEL MUSIC LISTENING TESTS

C.3 [musical notation: bass clef]

C.4 1980s

D.1 ascending major scale, ends on the dominant

D.2 glissando

D.3 28

D.4 descending walking bass

AoS 6: Contemporary traditional music

A.1 [musical notation: treble clef with two flats]

[1 mark for each of 2 correct accidentals added]

A.2 either of sitar [1] or tabla [1] [maximum 1 mark]

A.3 any of cello [1], double bass [1], violin [1] or synthesiser [1] [maximum 1 mark]

A.4 alap

B.1 fado

B.2 bar 1: ivb; bar 4: VII

B.3 augmented 6th

B.4 **A** is correct

C.1 any two of tambor, chicharra, latigo

C.2 arrestre

C.3 $\frac{4}{4}$

C.4 i – vb – VI – V

D.1 either of birimtingo or kumbengo

D.2 conjunct

D.3 tempo doubles/quickens [1]; pulse goes from triple to compound duple time ($\frac{3}{4}$ to $\frac{6}{8}$) [1]

D.4 one of the players knocks on the wood of their kora/percussive signal or similar answer

AoS 7: Art music since 1910

A.1 [musical notation: bass clef with flats, 4/4]

A.2 major

A.3 any of largo; lento; adagio; grave

A.4 violin and viola

B.1 [musical notation: rhythm]

[1 mark for each of 3 correct beats added]

B.2 6 times

B.3 any of: goes out of sync/phase [1]; cross-rhythm used [1] [maximum 1 mark]

C.1 minor 7th

C.2 bassoon

C.3 minor 7th chord

C.4 violin

C.5 glissando

D.1 any 2 of: use of pedal; very low register; pp/quiet; ascending then descending chromatic scales [maximum 2 marks]

D.2 slurred followed by staccato/detached [no marks for just one of these; maximum 1 mark]

D.3 flutter tonguing

D.4 **A** is correct

Track listings and copyrights

Track	Composer/ Artist	Piece	Label	Timings	Mechanical copyright
AS paper					
1	Bach	BWV 1056 in G, Mvt 1	Naxos 8.554169	0:00–0:33	
2	Mozart	*Don Giovanni* Act 2 Scene 15	Naxos 8.557893	0:00–0:32	
3	Mozart	*Magic Flute* Act 2 no. 13	Naxos 8.660030-31	0:00–0:28	
4a	Handel	Oboe concerto no. 2 mvt 2	Naxos 8.553430	0:00–0:31	
4b	Mozart	*Idomeneo* Act 1 Scene 1	Naxos 8.660250-52	0:00–0:49	
5	Stevie Wonder	'My cherie amour'	Motown	0:00–0:57	My Cherie Amour (Wonder/Cosby/Moy) EMI Music/Jobete Music/ EMI Music Publishing Ltd
6	Muse	'MK Ultra'	Warner Bros	1:02–1:58	MK Ultra (Bellamy) Warner/Chappell Music Publishing Limited
7	Daft Punk	'Instant crush'	Columbia	0:00–0:43	Instant Crush (Homem-Christo/Bangalter/Casablancas) Imagem Music/Julian Casablancas
8	Beyoncé	'Halo'	Columbia	2:01–3:52	Halo (Knowles/Bogart/Tedder) EMI Music Publishing Ltd/Sony/ATV Music Publishing (UK) Limited/ Downtown Music Publishing LLC
9	Thomas Newman	'Miss Wichita' from *Erin Brockovich*	Sony Music Entertainment	0:00–0:52	Miss Wichita (Newman) Sony/ATV Music Publishing (UK) Limited
10	Bernard Herrmann	'Memory Waltz' from *The snows of Kilimanjaro*	Silva Screen, Citizen Kane: The Essential Bernard Herrmann Film Music	0:00–0:30	Memory Waltz (Herrmann) EMI United Partnership Ltd
11	Hans Zimmer	'You're so cool' from *True Romance*	Morgan Creek Records	0:00–0:51	You're So Cool (Zimmer) Kobalt Music Publishing Limited

AS/A LEVEL MUSIC LISTENING TESTS

12	Michael Giacchino	'Laboratory Hunt' from *The Lost World: Jurassic Park* (Play-station)	SIR Digital	0:00–0:56	Laboratory Hunt (Giacchino) Warner/Chappell Artemis Music Limited
13	Rodgers	'People will say we're in love' from *Oklahoma!*	First Night Records	0:25–1:01	People Will Say We're In Love (Rodgers/Hammerstein) Rodgers & Hammerstein Theatrical Europe Ltd
14	Sondheim	'Send in the clowns' from *A little night music*	Masterworks Broadway	0:22–0:49	Send In The Clowns (Sondheim) Warner/Chappell North America Limited
15	Weill	'Wrapped in a ribbon and tied in a bow' from *Street scene*	Masterworks Broadway	0:00–0:25	Wrapped in a Ribbon and Tied in a Bow (Langston/Weill) Warner/Chappell North America Limited
16	Schoenberg	'Confront-ation' from *Les Misérables*	First Night Records	0:45–1:42	The Confrontation (Kretzmer/Boublil/Schonberg) Warner/Chappell North America Limited
17	Duke Ellington	'Take the A train'	Columbia Records/Sony	0:00–0:50	Take the A-Train (Strayhorn) Campbell Connelly And Co Ltd
18	Miles Davis	'Move'	Capitol Records	0:00–0:38	Move (Best) Campbell Connelly And Co Ltd
19	Charlie Parker	'Ornith-ology'	Naxos Jazz Legends 8.120571	0:00–0:40	Ornithology (Harris/Parker) Universal Music Publishing Limited
20	Pat Metheny	'Spring ain't here'	Nonesuch	0:00–1:25	Spring Ain't Here (Metheny) Kobalt Music Publishing Limited
21	Bellowhead	'Jordan'	Westpark	1:11–1:40	Jordan (Boden) Faber Music Ltd
22	Mariza	'Rosa Branca'	Parlophone	0:00–0:50	Rosa Branca (Dias/Guimaraes) Resende Dias/Jose De Jesus Guimaraes
23	Anoushka Shankar	'Reunion'	Deutsche Grammophon	1:00–1:45	Reunion (Shankar) Sony/ATV Music Publishing (UK) Limited/Chester Music

AS/A LEVEL MUSIC LISTENING TESTS

24	Toumani Diabaté's Symmetric Orchestra	'Ya Fama'	Nonesuch, World Circuit	0:00–1:15	Ya Fama (Diabaté) BMG Rights Management (UK) Limited
25	Vivaldi	Concerto in D op. 10 mvt 1	Naxos 8.554053	1:48–2:43	
26	Mozart	*Le nozze di Figaro* Act 1 no. 6	Naxos 8.660102-04	0:00–0:24	

AS additional dictation questions

27	Mozart	'Una bella serenata' from *Cosi fan tutte*	Naxos 8.553172	0:10–0:26	
28	Mozart	*Don Giovanni* Act 1 Scene 9	Naxos 8.557893	1:29–1:43	
29	Handel	Oboe concerto no. 2, mvt 3	Naxos 8.553430	0:36–0:56	

AS additional section B questions

30	Purcell	Trumpet sonata mvt 1, Allegro	Naxos 8.553444	0:00–0:39	
31	Mozart	*Le nozze di Figaro* Act 1, nos. 2 and 3, Recitative and Cavatina	Naxos 8.660102-04	1:44 – end and 0:00–0:18	

A Level paper

32	Grieg	'Wedding day at Troldhaugen'	Deutsche Grammophon Pletnev Grieg Lyric Pieces Op.65	0:00–0:55	
33	Handel	Oboe concerto no. 3 mvt 1	Naxos 8.553430	0:31–0:46	
34	Mozart	'Fin ch'han dal vino' from *Don Giovanni* Act 1	Naxos 8.557893	0:00–0:50	
35	Joni Mitchell	'California'	Reprise Records 7599-27199-2	1:14–2:05	Blue (Mitchell) 36Sony/ATV Music Publishing (UK) Limited
36	Labrinth	'Let the sun shine'	Syco Music 88691955162	0:00–1:13	Let The Sun Shine (McKenzie) EMI Music Publishing Ltd

AS/A LEVEL MUSIC LISTENING TESTS

37	Stevie Wonder	'Master Blaster (Jammin')'	Motown 530 044-2	2:30–3:52	Master Blaster (Wonder) EMI Music Publishing Ltd
38	Hans Zimmer	'Brothers' from *Backdraft*	Milan CD CH 807	0:00–0:47	Brothers (Zimmer) Universal/MCA Music Limited
39	Michael Giacchino	'C4-titude' from *Lost* season 4	Varèse Sarabande VSD-6964	0:00–0:53	C4-Titude (Giacchino) Warner/Chappell Artemis Music Limited
40	Bernard Herrmann	'Gort – The Visor' from *The day the earth stood still*	Twentieth Century Fox Film Scores 07822 11010 2	0:00–1.23	Gort / The Visor / The Telescope (Herrmann) EMI Music Publishing Ltd
41	Jason Robert Brown	'See I'm smiling' from *The last five years*	Ghostlight	0:05–0:23	See I'm Smiling (Brown) Semolina Farfalle Music Co
42	Rodgers	'Some enchanted evening' from *South Pacific*	First Night Records	0:25–1:03	Some Enchanted Evening (Rodgers/Hammerstein) Rodgers & Hammerstein Theatrical Europe Ltd
43	Schoenberg	'Why God, why?' from *Miss Saigon*	Polydor Group	0:10–1:30	Why God, Why? (Boublil/Schonberg/Boublil) Warner/Chappell North America Limited
44	The Impossible Gentlemen	'Barber Blues'	BASHO	0:00–0:38	Barber Blues (Simcock) Gwilym Raymond Simcock
45	Duke Ellington	'In a sentimental mood'	Columbia Records/Sony	0:00–0:40	In a Sentimental Mood (Mills/Kurtz/Ellington) Lafleur Music Ltd
46	Miles Davis	'Summer-time'	Columbia Legacy	0:00–1:18	Summertime (Heyward/Gershwin/Gershwin) Warner/Chappell North America Limited/Ira Gershwin
47	Ali Farka Touré and Toumani Diabaté	'Ruby'	World Circuit WLWCD083	0:12–0:51	Ruby (Touré) Kobalt Music Publishing Limited
48	Astor Piazzolla	'Adios Nonino'	Alfa Records AFCD-13	0:00–0:44	Adios Nonino (Piazzolla) Warner Chappell Overseas Holdings Limited/Astor Pantaleon Piazzolla

AS/A LEVEL MUSIC LISTENING TESTS

49	Bellowhead	'A-begging I will go'	Navigator Records NAVIGATOR 042X	0:00–1:36	A-Begging I Will Go (Trad/Boden) Jonathan James Boden
50	Steve Reich	Four Organs	Nonesuch	3:11–3:34	Four Organs (Reich) Universal Edition (London) Ltd
51	Shostakovich	Jazz suite no. 2, 'Little polka'	Naxos 555949	0:00–0:24	Jazz Suite No 2 (Shostakovich) Boosey-And-Hawkes-Music-Publ-Ltd/Dmitrij Dmitrievich Shostakovich
52	James MacMillan	'Birthday present,	Decca (UMO)	0:00–1:11	Birthday Present (MacMillan) Boosey-And-Hawkes-Music-Publ-Ltd
53	Vivaldi	Concerto in D op. 10 mvt 3	Naxos 8.554053	0:00–0:33	
54	Mozart	*Le nozze di Figaro* Act 1 no. 1	Naxos 8.660102-04	0:00–1:24	
55	Brahms	Intermezzo in A major op. 118 no. 2	Naxos 8.550354	0:00–0:52	

A Level additional dictation questions

56	Vivaldi	'Spring' mvt 3	Naxos 8.553219	0:48–1:01	
57	Chopin	Mazurka op. 33 no. 4	Naxos 8.550358	3:52–4:20	
58	Mozart	*The Magic Flute* no. 3	Naxos 8.660030-31	0:00–0:32	

A Level additional section B questions

59	Bach	Violin concerto 1041 mvt 3	Naxos 8.554603	0:00–1:02	
60	Mozart	*Le nozze di Figaro* Overture	Naxos 8.660102-04	0:00–0:48	
61	Grieg	'Norwegian march' op. 54 no. 2	Naxos 8.553395	0:00–1:19	

Additional optional Areas of Study questions

62	Joni Mitchell	'The circle game'	Reprise Records 244 085	0:00–0:44	The Circle Game (Mitchell) Westminster Music Ltd

AS/A LEVEL MUSIC LISTENING TESTS

63	Beyoncé	'Broken-hearted girl'	Music World Music 88697 61433 2	0:58–1:55	Broken-Hearted Girl (Knowles/Eriksen/Edmonds/Hermansen) EMI Music Publishing Ltd/Sony/ATV Music Publishing (UK) Limited/Universal/MCA Music Limited
64	Daft Punk	'Lose yourself to dance'	Columbia 88883716862	1:15–2:15	Lose Yourself To Dance (Williams/Rodgers/Bangalter/Homem-Christo) EMI Music Publishing Ltd/Sony/ATV Music Publishing (UK) Limited/Imagem Music
65	Labrinth feat. Tinie Tempah	Earthquake (radio edit)	Sony Music G010002714782Y	0:27–1:12	Earthquake (feat Tinie Tempah) (Roberts/Okogwu/McKenzie) EMI Music Publishing Ltd
66	Thomas Newman	'Exclusion zone' from *The iron lady*	Sony Classical 88697978942	0:58–1:34	Exclusion Zone (Newman) Children of Thirteen Music
67	Nobuo Uematsu	'In search of the ruins', *Blue Dragon*	Sumthing Else Music Works B003TKZHS8	0:00–1:00	In Search of the Ruins (Uematsu) Universal/MCA Music Limited
68	Bernard Herrmann	'The hotel room' from *Marnie*	Tsunami TCI 0601	0:00–0:51	Hotel Room (Herrmann) Bourne Music Ltd
69	Thomas Newman	'Foolish-ment' from *The green mile*	Warner Bros. Records 9 47584-2	0:00–0:45	Foolishment (Newman) Universal Music Publishing Limited
70	Weill	'What good would the moon be?' from *Street Scene*	Masterworks Broadway	0:37–1:13	How Good Would The Moon Be (Langston/Weill) Warner/Chappell North America Limited
71	Schoenberg	'Drink with me' from *Les misérables*	First Night Records	0:19–0:51	Drink With Me (Boublil/Schonberg/Kretzmer) Warner/Chappell North America Limited
72	Rodgers	'My favourite things' from *Sound Of Music*	Really Useful Group	0:00–0:28	My Favourite Things (Rodgers/Hammerstein) Rodgers & Hammerstein Theatrical Europe Ltd
73	Jason Robert Brown	'I can do better than that' from *The last five years*	Ghostlight	0:00–0:39	I Can Do Better Than That (Brown) Semolina Farfalle Music Co

AS/A LEVEL MUSIC LISTENING TESTS

74	Gwilym Simcock	'Above the sun'	Act Music	0:22–1:24	Above The Sun (Garland) Copyright Control
75	Miles Davis	'Walkin''	Prestige records	0:50–1:24	Walkin' (Carpenter) EMI United Partnership Ltd
76	Pat Metheny	'Chris'	EMI America Records	0:00–0:49	Chris (Mays/Metheny) Sony/ATV Music Publishing (UK) Limited
77	Louis Armstrong	'Struttin' with some barbecue'	JSP	0:00–0:35	Struttin' With Some Barbecue (Armstrong) Universal/MCA Music Limited
78	Anoushka Shankar	'Boat to nowhere'	Deutsche Grammophon 4795459	1:20–2:21	Boat To Nowhere (Delago/Shankar/Hepple) Copyright Control/ Manu Delago
79	Mariza	'Medo'	Parlophone 2564631532	1:20–2:02	Medo (Oulman/Ferreira) Alain Robert Bertrand Oulman/Reinaldo Edgar De Azevedo Silva Ferreira
80	Astor Piazzolla	'Primavera Porteña'	BMG BVCM-38056	0:00–1:15	Primavera Portena (Piazzolla) Warner Chappell Overseas Holdings Limited/Astor Pantaleon Piazzolla
81	Ballaké Sissoko and Toumani Diabaté	'Kora Bali'	Hannibal Records HNCD1428	2:58–3:54	Kora Bali (Diabate) BMG Rights Management (UK) Limited
82	Shostakovich	String quartet no. 8 mvt 1	Naxos 8.550973	0:00–0:53	String Quartet No 8 in C Minor Op 110 (Shostakovich) Boosey & Hawkes Music Publishers Ltd/Dmitrij Dmitrievich Shostakovich
83	Steve Reich	'Clapping music'	LSO Live	0:00–0:21	Clapping Music (Reich) Universal Edition (London) Ltd
84	MacMillan	Oboe concerto mvt 1	Harmonia mundi	0:00–0:50	Oboe Concerto (MacMillan) Boosey & Hawkes Music Publishers Ltd
85	Messiaen	'Le merle noir'	Naxos 8.557328	0:00–0:49	Le Merle Noir (Messiaen) © Copyright 1952 Alphonse Leduc, Paris All Rights Reserved. International Copyright Secured.

AS/A LEVEL MUSIC LISTENING TESTS

Printed music copyrights

My Cherie Amour
Words and music by Stevie Wonder, Henry Cosby & Sylvia Moy. © Copyright 1968 (Renewed 1996) Jobete Music Company Incorporated, USA/Stone Agate Music, USA/Sawandi Music, USA/Black Bull Music Incorporated, USA. EMI Music/Jobete Music/EMI Music Publishing Limited. All Rights Reserved. International Copyright Secured.

MK Ultra
Words and music by Matthew Bellamy. © Copyright 2009 Loosechord Limited. Warner/Chappell Music Limited. All Rights Reserved. International Copyright Secured.

Instant Crush
Words and music by Thomas Bangalter, Guy-Manuel de Homem-Christo & Julian Casablancas. © Copyright 2013 Imagem Music BV. Imagem Music /Julian Casablancas. All Rights Reserved. International Copyright Secured.

Halo
Words and music by Ryan Tedder, Beyoncé Knowles & Evan Bogart. © Copyright 2008 Sony/ATV Songs LLC/EMI April Music Incorporated/Write 2 Live Publishing/B Day Publishing/Here's Lookin At You Kidd Music. EMI Music Publishing Limited/Sony/ATV Music Publishing (UK) Limited/Downtown Music Publishing LLC. All Rights Reserved. International Copyright Secured.

Erin Brockovich
Music by Thomas Newman. © Copyright 2000 Colpix Music Inc. Sony/ATV Music Publishing. All Rights Reserved. International Copyright Secured.

Memory Waltz (From *The Snows Of Kilimanjaro*)
Music by Bernard Herrmann. © Copyright 1952 EMI Robbins Catalog Inc. EMI United Partnership Limited. All Rights Reserved. International Copyright Secured.

People Will Say We're In Love (From *Oklahoma!*)
Words by Oscar Hammerstein II, music by Richard Rodgers. © Copyright 1943 Williamson Music Company, USA. Rodgers & Hammerstein Theatrical Europe Limited. Print Rights administered by Hal Leonard LLC. All Rights Reserved. International Copyright Secured.

Send In The Clowns (from *A Little Night Music*)
Words and music by Stephen Sondheim. © Copyright 1973 Rilting Music Inc. Print Rights administered by Hal Leonard LLC. All Rights Reserved. International Copyright Secured.

Wrapped In A Ribbon And Tied With A Bow (from *Street Scene*)
Words by Hughes Langston, music by Kurt Weill. © Copyright 1946 Kurt Weill Foundation For Music/Chappell-Co Inc. Warner/Chappell North America Limited. All Rights Reserved. International Copyright Secured.

Take The 'A' Train
Words and music by Billy Strayhorn. © Copyright 1941 Music Sales Corporation/Tempo Music Inc. Administered by Chester Music Limited trading as Campbell Connelly & Co for the British Reversionary Territories. All Rights Reserved. International Copyright Secured.

Ornithology
Music by Charlie Parker and Benny Harris. © Copyright 1946 Atlantic Music Corporation, USA. Universal Music Publishing Limited. All Rights Reserved. International Copyright Secured.

Jordan
Traditional. Arranged by Frankie Armstrong. © Copyright 1971 Fellsongs Publishing. All Rights Reserved. International Copyright Secured.

California
Words and music by Joni Mitchell. © Copyright 1971 Joni Mitchell Publishing Corporation, USA. Sony/ATV Music Publishing. All Rights Reserved. International Copyright Secured.

Let The Sun Shine
Words and music by Timothy McKenzie. © Copyright 2010 Stellar Songs Limited. EMI Music Publishing Limited. All Rights Reserved. International Copyright Secured.

C4-Titude (from *Lost: Season 4*)
Music by Michael Giacchino. © Copyright 2008 Touchstone Pictures Music & Songs Incorporated, USA. Warner/Chappell Artemis Music Limited. All Rights Reserved. International Copyright Secured.

See, I'm Smiling (from *The Last Five Years*)
Words and music by Jason Robert Brown. © Copyright 2001 Semolina Farfalle Music Company. All Rights Reserved. International Copyright Secured.

Some Enchanted Evening (from *South Pacific*)
Words by Oscar Hammerstein II, music by Richard Rodgers. © Copyright 1949 (Renewed) Williamson Music Company. Rodgers & Hammerstein Theatrical Europe Limited. Print Rights administered by Hal Leonard LLC. All Rights Reserved. International Copyright Secured.

Why God Why? (from *Miss Saigon*)
Music by Claude-Michel Schönberg, lyrics by Alain Boublil & Richard Maltby Jr. Adapted from Original Lyrics by Alain Boublil. © Copyright (Music & French Lyrics) 1987, (English Lyrics) 1988, (Additional Music & Lyrics) 1989 Alain Boublil Music Limited. All Rights Reserved. International Copyright Secured. For the UK and Eire, Alain Boublil Overseas Limited.

Barber Blues
Music by Gwilym Raymond Simcock. © Copyright 2013 Gwilym Simcock. All Rights Reserved. International Copyright Secured.

AS/A LEVEL MUSIC LISTENING TESTS

In A Sentimental Mood
Words and music by Duke Ellington, Irving Mills
& Manny Kurtz. © Copyright 1935 EMI Mills Music Inc.
Lafleur Music Limited. All Rights Reserved.
International Copyright Secured.

A-Begging I Will Go
Traditional. Arranged by Jonathan Boden.
© Copyright 2010 Jonathan Boden. All Rights Reserved.
International Copyright Secured.

Four Organs
Music by Steve Reich. © Copyright 1970 Universal
Edition (London) Limited. All Rights Reserved.
International Copyright Secured.

The Circle Game
Words and music by Joni Mitchell. © Copyright 1970
Gandalf Publishing. Westminster Music Limited.
All Rights Reserved. International Copyright Secured.

Broken-hearted Girl
Words and music by Kenneth 'Babyface' Edmonds,
Mikkel S. Eriksen, Tor Erik Hermansen & Beyoncé
Knowles. © Copyright 2009 Songs Of Universal
Incorporated/Faze 2 Music/Sony/ATV Music Publishing
LLC/B-Day Publishing/EMI April Music Inc. Universal/
MCA Music Limited/EMI Music Publishing Limited/
Sony/ATV Music Publishing. All Rights Reserved.
International Copyright Secured.

Lose Yourself To Dance
Words and music by Thomas Bangalter, Pharrell Williams,
Guy-Manuel de Homem-Christo and Nile Rodgers.
© Copyright 2013 EMI April Music Inc/Imagem CV/More
Water From Nazareth Publishing, Inc. Imagem Music/
Sony/ATV Music Publishing/EMI Music Publishing Ltd.
All Rights Reserved. International Copyright Secured.

In Search Of The Ruins (from *Blue Dragon*)
Music by Nobuo Uematsu. © Copyright 2006 Aniplex
Incorporated. Sony/ATV Music Publishing.
All Rights Reserved. International Copyright Secured.

What Good Would The Moon Be? (from *Street Scene*)
Words by Hughes Langston, music by Kurt Weill.
© Copyright 1946 Kurt Weill Foundation For Music/
Chappell-Co Inc. Warner/Chappell North America
Limited. All Rights Reserved. International Copyright
Secured.

Drink With Me (From *Les Misérables*)
Music by Claude-Michel Schönberg, lyrics by
Alain Boublil & Herbert Kretzmer. © Copyright 1985
(Music & Lyrics) Alain Boublil Music Limited (ASCAP).
All Rights Reserved. International Copyright Secured.

My Favourite Things (from *The Sound Of Music*)
Words by Oscar Hammerstein II, music by Richard
Rodgers. © Copyright 1959 (Renewed) Richard Rodgers
and Oscar Hammerstein II. Williamson Music, a Division
of Rodgers & Hammerstein: an Imagem Company, owner
of publication and allied rights throughout the world.
Print Rights administered by Hal Leonard LLC.
All Rights Reserved. International Copyright Secured.

Chris
Words and music by Pat Metheny & Lyle Mays.
© Copyright Pat Meth Music Corporation, USA/
Donna Dijon Music Publication. Sony/ATV Music
Publishing. All Rights Reserved. International
Copyright Secured.

Boat To Nowhere
Words by Julian Kenneth Joseph Hepple and Manu
Delago, music by Anoushka Shankar, Julian Kenneth
Joseph Hepple and Manu Delago. © Copyright 2016
St Rose Music Publishing Co/Anourag Music Publishing
Chester Music Limited/Copyright Contol/Delago Manu.
All Rights Reserved. International Copyright Secured.

Medo
Words by Reinaldo Ferreira, music by Alain Oulman.
© Copyright Copyright Control. All Rights Reserved.
International Copyright Secured.

String Quartet No. 8
Music by Dmitri Shostakovich. © Copyright 1960
Boosey & Hawkes Music Publishers Ltd. All Rights
Reserved. International Copyright Secured.

Clapping Music
Music by Steve Reich. © Copyright 1972 Universal
Edition (London) Limited. All Rights Reserved.
International Copyright Secured.

Le Merle Noir
Music by Oliver Messiaen. © Copyright 1952
Alphonse Leduc, Paris. All Rights Reserved.
International Copyright Secured.